I0408829

Ernesto Cira

Binance Trading Guide: A Comprehensive Guide to Thriving in the Cryptocurrency Market.

Copyright © 2023 by Ernesto Cira

All rights reserved. No part of this publication may be reproduced, stored or transmitted in any form or by any means, electronic, mechanical, photocopying, recording, scanning, or otherwise without written permission from the publisher. It is illegal to copy this book, post it to a website, or distribute it by any other means without permission.

Ernesto Cira asserts the moral right to be identified as the author of this work.

First edition

This book was professionally typeset on Reedsy
Find out more at reedsy.com

"Dedicated to the pioneers of the digital frontier, forging new paths in the world of cryptocurrencies. Your courage and curiosity inspire us all to explore the future of finance."

Contents

    1.

    2.

    3.

    4.

    5.

    6.

    7.

    8.

9.

10.

11.

12.

13.

Preface

Welcome to "Binance Trading Guide: A Comprehensive Guide to Thriving in the Cryptocurrency Market." In this rapidly evolving digital landscape, the world of cryptocurrency has emerged as a force to be reckoned with. Cryptocurrencies, powered by blockchain technology, have redefined finance, offering new opportunities and challenges for investors and traders alike.

This book is your compass in the complex and exciting terrain of cryptocurrency trading, with a special focus on the renowned Binance exchange. Whether you're an experienced trader looking to sharpen your skills or someone brand new to the world of cryptocurrencies, we've designed this guide to provide you with the knowledge, strategies, and insights you need to thrive.

Our journey begins with a solid foundation in cryptocurrency fundamentals, ensuring that you understand the technology, terminology, and market dynamics. From there, we dive deep into the art and science of trading, offering proven strategies and techniques for managing risk, making informed decisions, and achieving your financial goals.

Navigating the Binance platform can be intimidating for newcomers, but fear not – we've got you covered. Our step-by-step instructions and insider tips will have you trading with confidence and efficiency in no time.

The world of cryptocurrency isn't just about Bitcoin and Ethereum. You'll also explore the vast universe of altcoins and tokens, discovering how to research, evaluate, and build a diversified portfolio that aligns with your goals.

But it's not all about gains and profits. In this guide, we'll also delve into the potential challenges and uncertainties of the cryptocurrency market, preparing you to face them head-on. We'll discuss security measures, regulatory considerations, and the psychological aspects of trading.

In this dynamic space, predictions and trends are ever-shifting. In the final chapter, we'll gaze into the crystal ball to explore what the future might hold for cryptocurrency trading and Binance. Anticipate innovations, challenges, and opportunities that lie ahead.

Remember, cryptocurrency trading is not a guaranteed path to riches, and it's not without risks. But with knowledge, discipline, and the insights shared in this guide, you'll be better equipped to navigate the exciting world of cryptocurrencies and increase your chances of success.

So, whether you're a seasoned trader or a curious newcomer, fasten your seatbelt and prepare for an enlightening journey into the world of cryptocurrency trading. "Binance Trading Guide" is your trusted companion on this thrilling ride.

Let's embark on this adventure together and discover the potential that the cryptocurrency market has to offer.

Happy Trading!

Ernesto   Cira

1

Introduction to Binance

What is Binance?

Binance is one of the world's largest and most popular cryptocurrency exchanges. It was founded in 2017 by Changpeng Zhao (often referred to as "CZ") and quickly gained prominence in the cryptocurrency industry. Binance offers a wide range of services related to cryptocurrencies, making it a comprehensive platform for both beginners and experienced cryptocurrency traders and investors. Here are some key aspects of what Binance is:

1. **Cryptocurrency Exchange:** At its core, Binance is a cryptocurrency exchange platform. It allows users to trade various cryptocurrencies for one another. Traders can buy and sell digital assets like Bitcoin, Ethereum, Ripple, and numerous other altcoins on the platform. Binance provides a user-friendly interface for executing trades and offers advanced trading features for more experienced users.

2. **Wide Range of Cryptocurrencies**: Binance offers a vast selection of cryptocurrencies for trading. While some exchanges

only provide a limited number of digital assets, Binance regularly adds new tokens and coins to its platform, providing traders with access to a diverse range of investment options.

3. **Binance Coin (BNB):** Binance has its native cryptocurrency called Binance Coin (BNB). BNB has various use cases within the Binance ecosystem, including reducing trading fees, participating in token sales on the Binance Launchpad, and more. BNB has gained popularity not only for its utility within the platform but also as an investment.

4. **Advanced Trading Features**: Binance caters to both novice and experienced traders. It offers features such as spot trading, margin trading, and futures trading. Users can take advantage of leverage and various order types to execute more advanced trading strategies.

5. **Security:** Binance places a strong emphasis on security. It employs industry-standard security practices like two-factor authentication (2FA) and cold storage for user funds to protect against hacks and unauthorized access.

6. **Additional Services**: In addition to trading, Binance provides various other services, including:

- **Binance Savings**: Allows users to earn interest on their cryptocurrency holdings by participating in savings products.

- Binance Staking: Users can stake certain cryptocurrencies to earn rewards or participate in network governance.

- Binance Launchpad: A platform for token sales and initial coin offerings (ICOs), where users can invest in new blockchain projects.

- Binance Academy: An educational platform offering cryptocurrency and blockchain-related courses and resources.

- Binance Card: A crypto debit card that allows users to spend their cryptocurrency holdings in the real world.

- Binance Research: Provides in-depth analysis and reports on various cryptocurrencies and blockchain projects.

7. **Global Presence**: Binance has a global presence and serves users from around the world. It offers support for multiple languages and provides customer support in various time zones.

Why use Binance for trading?

Using Binance for trading has several advantages that make it a popular choice among cryptocurrency traders. Here are some key reasons why you should use Binance for trading:

1. **Liquidity**: Binance is known for its high liquidity, which means there are usually plenty of buyers and sellers in the market. This liquidity can result in narrower bid-ask spreads and less price slippage, making it easier for traders to execute their orders at desired prices.

2. **User-Friendly Interface:** Binance provides a user-friendly trading platform that caters to both beginners and experienced traders. The interface is intuitive and offers various trading views, including a basic mode for beginners and an advanced mode for more experienced traders who use technical analysis.

3. **Low Fees**: Binance typically charges lower trading fees compared to many other cryptocurrency exchanges. Users can further reduce fees by holding Binance Coin (BNB) and using it to pay for trading fees. This fee reduction can make a significant difference for active traders.

4. **Security Measures**: Binance places a strong emphasis on security. They employ industry-standard security practices, including two-factor authentication (2FA) and cold storage for the majority of user funds. Binance also has a bug bounty program to incentivize the discovery and reporting of vulnerabilities.

5. **Access to Additional Services:** In addition to spot trading, Binance offers various other services such as futures and options trading, staking, savings, and launchpad for new token offerings. These services provide traders with additional ways to engage with cryptocurrencies and potentially earn profits.

6. **Binance Coin (BNB)**: Binance has its native cryptocurrency, Binance Coin (BNB), which has various use cases within the Binance ecosystem. Users can use BNB to pay for trading fees at a discount, participate in token sales on the Binance Launchpad, and more.

7. **Global Presence:** Binance has a global presence and offers its services to users in many countries around the world. This accessibility makes it a popular choice for traders in different regions.

8. **Customer Support:** Binance provides customer support through various channels, including a help centre, live chat, and a support ticket system. This can be crucial for users who encounter issues or have questions related to their accounts.

9. **Innovative Features**: Binance is known for its continuous innovation, regularly adding new features and trading options. This keeps traders engaged and allows them to adapt to changing market conditions.

A brief history of Binance:

Foundation and Early Years (2017):

- Binance was founded by Changpeng Zhao (CZ), a well-known figure in the cryptocurrency space, in July 2017.

- The company's initial coin offering (ICO) for its native cryptocurrency, Binance Coin (BNB), raised $15 million in just a few weeks.

- Binance launched its cryptocurrency exchange platform in July 2017, initially headquartered in China. However, it soon moved its operations to Japan due to regulatory concerns in China.

Rapid Growth and Expansion (2017-2018):

- Binance quickly gained popularity in the cryptocurrency community for its low trading fees, a wide range of supported cryptocurrencies, and a user-friendly interface.

- Within just a few months of its launch, Binance became one of the largest cryptocurrency exchanges in the world by trading volume.

- In early 2018, Binance introduced its blockchain called Binance Chain and the Binance DEX (decentralized exchange) to facilitate peer-to-peer trading.

- Binance also continued to expand its services, introducing Binance Launchpad, which allowed blockchain projects to raise funds through token sales on the platform.

Challenges and Hacks (2019):

- Despite its rapid success, Binance faced challenges in 2019. In May of that year, it experienced a significant security breach in which hackers stole over 7,000 Bitcoins (BTC) from the exchange.

- CZ and the Binance team responded swiftly by covering the losses from the exchange's SAFU (Secure Asset Fund for Users) fund, which was established to protect user funds.

Global Regulatory Challenges (2020-2021):

- Binance continued to grow in 2020, expanding its services, including the launch of Binance.US to cater to the American market.

- However, in 2021, Binance faced increased regulatory scrutiny in several countries, with some regulators raising concerns about its compliance with local laws and regulations.

- This led Binance to make adjustments to its services in various regions, including discontinuing services like futures and options trading in certain countries.

Diverse Offerings and Innovations (2021-2022):

- Despite regulatory challenges, Binance continued to innovate and expand its offerings. It introduced features like Binance Smart Chain (BSC), a blockchain platform that allowed for the creation of decentralized applications (DApps).

- Binance also expanded into non-fungible tokens (NFTs) and launched NFT marketplaces, allowing users to buy, sell, and trade digital collectables.

- CZ and the Binance team remained committed to improving security and compliance measures to address regulatory concerns and maintain user trust.

Ongoing Evolution (2023 and Beyond):

- The future of Binance remained uncertain, with the company actively working to adapt to changing regulatory landscapes and market dynamics.

- Binance's history is marked by its ability to pivot and adapt quickly to challenges and opportunities, so the company will likely continue to evolve and expand its services in the years to come.

Getting started with Binance: Sign-up and verification:

Step 1: Visit the Binance Website

- Begin by visiting the official Binance website *(www.binance.com)* using a web browser on your computer or mobile device.

Step 2: Click on "Register"

- On the Binance homepage, you'll typically find a "Register" or "Sign up" button. Click on it to initiate the registration process.

Step 3: Enter Your Email and Password

- You will be prompted to enter your email address and create a strong, secure password. Follow the password requirements specified by Binance (e.g., a combination of letters, numbers, and special characters).

Step 4: Agree to the Terms of Use

- Carefully read Binance's Terms of Use and Privacy Policy. Make sure you understand and agree to their terms and conditions before proceeding.

Step 5: Solve the CAPTCHA

- Complete any CAPTCHA verification required to prove that you are not a robot. This step is essential for security.

Step 6: Click "Register"

- Once you've filled out the necessary information and agreed to the terms, click the "Register" button to create your account.

Step 7: Email Verification

- Check the email address you provided during registration. Binance will send you a verification email. Open your email inbox and find the message from Binance.

Step 8: Verify Your Email

- Open the verification email and click on the verification link or button provided in the email. This confirms your email address with Binance.

Step 9: Enable Two-Factor Authentication (2FA)

- For added security, it's highly recommended to enable Two-Factor Authentication (2FA). You can choose to use a mobile app like Google Authenticator or receive codes via SMS.

Step 10: Log into Your Binance Account

- Go back to the Binance website and log in using your email address and the password you created during registration.

Step 11: Complete Identity Verification (KYC)

- Depending on your region and the features you wish to use, you may be required to complete identity verification (KYC). This typically involves providing personal information and uploading identification documents like a passport or driver's license.

- To complete KYC, go to your account settings and look for the "Identity Verification" or "KYC Verification" section. Follow the instructions provided to submit the required documents.

Step 12: Wait for Verification

- After submitting your KYC documents, Binance will review your information. This process may take some time, so be patient.

Step 13: Start Trading

- Once your identity verification is approved, you can start trading on Binance. You can deposit funds into your account and begin exploring the various cryptocurrency markets and trading pairs offered by the platform.

It's important to note that Binance's specific sign-up and verification process may evolve, and requirements can vary based on your location and intended use of the platform. Always follow the instructions provided on the Binance website and stay informed about any updates to their procedures and security measures.

2

Cryptocurrency Basics

Understanding cryptocurrencies:

Cryptocurrencies have emerged as a groundbreaking innovation in the realm of finance, offering a decentralized, transparent, and secure alternative to traditional monetary systems. In this chapter, we will embark on a journey to explore the fundamental concepts and intricacies of cryptocurrencies, setting the stage for informed and confident trading on platforms like Binance.

1. Introduction to Cryptocurrencies

At its core, cryptocurrency is a form of digital or virtual currency that leverages cryptographic techniques to secure transactions and control the creation of new units. Unlike traditional currencies issued and regulated by governments (fiat currencies), cryptocurrencies operate on decentralized networks, with no central authority governing them. This decentralized nature is a defining characteristic of cryptocurrencies and sets them apart from conventional financial systems.

2. How Cryptocurrencies Work

Central to the functioning of cryptocurrencies is blockchain technology. A blockchain is a distributed ledger that records all transactions across a network of computers. Transactions are grouped into blocks and linked together in chronological order. Each block contains a cryptographic reference to the previous block, creating a secure and immutable chain of data. This transparency and immutability ensure the integrity of the transaction history, making it nearly impossible to alter or counterfeit.

In addition to the blockchain, cryptography plays a pivotal role in securing cryptocurrencies. Private and public keys are used to facilitate transactions. The public key, akin to a bank account number, is openly shared and identifies the recipient of funds, while the private key, like a PIN or password, is kept secret and used to authorize transactions. Cryptography ensures that only the rightful owner of a private key can access and control their cryptocurrency holdings.

3. Key Characteristics of Cryptocurrencies

a. **Digital Nature**:

Cryptocurrencies exist purely in digital form, lacking a physical counterpart like paper money or coins. They are stored in digital wallets, which can be software-based (online) or hardware-based (offline).

b. **Transparency:** Blockchain technology enables anyone to access and view the entire transaction history of a cryptocurrency. This transparency fosters trust among users and eliminates the need for intermediaries like banks.

c. *Anonymity vs. Pseudonymity:* While cryptocurrencies provide a degree of privacy through pseudonymous addresses (represented by strings of characters), they are not entirely anonymous. Every transaction is recorded on the blockchain, potentially enabling forensic analysis.

d. **Limited Supply:** Many cryptocurrencies, including Bitcoin, have a capped supply. For example, Bitcoin's maximum supply is 21 million coins. This scarcity can influence its value over time.

4. Utility and Use Cases

Cryptocurrencies serve a multitude of purposes:

a. **Digital Gold**: Bitcoin is often likened to digital gold due to its store of value properties. Some view it as a hedge against inflation and economic instability.

b. *Peer-to-Peer Payments*: Cryptocurrencies offer a fast and cost-effective way to transfer funds globally without relying on traditional banks or payment processors.

c. **Smart Contracts**: Ethereum, a cryptocurrency with a strong focus on smart contracts, enables the creation of self-executing contracts with predefined rules and conditions.

d. *ICOs and Tokenization*: Cryptocurrencies have facilitated fundraising through Initial Coin Offerings (ICOs) and the tokenization of assets, such as real estate and art.

5. Popular Cryptocurrencies

a. **Bitcoin (BTC):** As the pioneer of cryptocurrencies, Bitcoin is synonymous with the crypto world. It was created by an anonymous person or group known as Satoshi Nakamoto and serves as digital gold.

b. **Ethereum (ETH):** Ethereum introduced the concept of smart contracts, expanding the utility of blockchain beyond simple transactions.

c. **Ripple (XRP), Litecoin (LTC), and Binance Coin (BNB):** These are among the many altcoins (alternative cryptocurrencies) that offer unique features and use cases.

6. Challenges and Concerns

While cryptocurrencies hold immense promise, they also face challenges and concerns:

a. **Price Volatility:** Cryptocurrency markets are known for their extreme price fluctuations, driven by factors such as market sentiment, news events, and speculative trading.

b. **Regulatory Concerns**: The regulatory landscape for cryptocurrencies varies widely by country, leading to uncertainty and potential legal risks for users.

c. **Security Risks**: Cryptocurrency holdings are susceptible to hacking and fraud. Secure storage methods, such as hardware wallets and strong passwords, are essential.

7. Future of Cryptocurrencies

The future of cryptocurrencies is a topic of intense speculation and innovation. Some key trends and developments include:

a. **Mainstream Adoption:** Cryptocurrencies are inching closer to mainstream acceptance, with increasing adoption by businesses and individuals.

b. **Decentralized Finance (DeFi)**: DeFi projects are disrupting traditional financial services like lending, borrowing, and trading, all on blockchain networks.

c. **Non-Fungible Tokens (NFTs)**: NFTs have gained prominence as unique digital assets representing ownership of digital art, collectables, and more.

D. **Scaling Solutions:** Ongoing efforts to improve blockchain scalability and reduce transaction costs are vital for broader adoption.

Different types of cryptocurrencies:

1. **Bitcoin (BTC):** Bitcoin is the first and most well-known cryptocurrency. It was created by an anonymous person or group of

people using the pseudonym Satoshi Nakamoto in 2009. Bitcoin is often referred to as digital gold and is primarily used as a store of value and a medium of exchange. It's characterized by its decentralized nature, security, and limited supply (21 million coins).

2. **Altcoins**: Altcoins are cryptocurrencies other than Bitcoin. They include a wide range of digital currencies, such as Ethereum (ETH), Ripple (XRP), Litecoin (LTC), and many others. Altcoins often have specific use cases or unique features that differentiate them from Bitcoin.

3. **Smart Contract Platforms**: Some cryptocurrencies, like Ethereum, are designed to support smart contracts. These are self-executing contracts with the terms of the agreement directly written into code. Smart contract platforms enable decentralized applications (DApps) to be built on top of their blockchain.

4. **Privacy Coins:** Privacy coins, such as Monero (XMR) and Zcash (ZEC), prioritize user anonymity and privacy. They use advanced cryptographic techniques to obscure transaction details, making it difficult to trace the flow of funds.

5. **Stablecoins:** Stablecoins like Tether (USDT), USD Coin (USDC), and DAI are designed to have a stable value, often pegged to a fiat currency like the US dollar. They are used as a bridge between cryptocurrencies and traditional financial systems, providing stability for traders and investors.

6. **Utility Tokens:** These tokens are created to serve a specific purpose within a particular blockchain ecosystem. For example, Binance Coin (BNB) is used to pay for transaction fees on the Binance exchange, and Chainlink (LINK) is used to facilitate data transfer between smart contracts and external sources.

7. **Security Tokens:** Security tokens represent ownership in an underlying asset, such as real estate or company shares. They are subject to securities regulations and can represent ownership, profit-sharing, or voting rights in the asset.

8. **Non-Fungible Tokens (NFTs):** NFTs are unique digital assets that represent ownership of a specific item, piece of art, collectable, or in-game item. They have gained significant attention for their use in digital art, gaming, and entertainment industries.

9. **Platform Coins:** Some cryptocurrencies serve as the native currency of a specific blockchain or platform. For example, NEO's GAS is used for transactions and computation on the NEO blockchain, while Ether (ETH) is used on the Ethereum platform.

10. **Community Coins:** These are often smaller cryptocurrencies with strong communities and niche use cases. They may be used for tipping content creators, supporting open-source projects, or promoting specific social causes.

It's important to note that the cryptocurrency landscape is highly dynamic, and new coins and tokens are constantly being created.

Investors and users should conduct thorough research before investing in or using any cryptocurrency to understand its purpose, technology, and potential risks. Additionally, regulatory environments for cryptocurrencies can vary by country, so compliance with local laws is crucial.

How blockchain technology works:

Blockchain technology is a decentralized and distributed ledger system that underlies most cryptocurrencies, including Bitcoin. It's a digital record-keeping system that allows multiple parties to maintain a secure and transparent record of transactions without the need for a centralized authority, such as a bank or government. Here's a more detailed explanation of how blockchain technology works:

1. **Decentralization:** Traditional financial systems rely on centralized authorities (e.g., banks, and governments) to validate and record transactions. In contrast, a blockchain is a decentralized network of computers, often referred to as nodes, that work together to validate and record transactions. There is no single point of control, making it resistant to censorship and tampering.

2. **Transactions:** Any activity on a blockchain starts with a transaction. Transactions can represent various activities, such as

transferring cryptocurrency, executing smart contracts, or recording ownership changes. Each transaction contains essential information, including sender and receiver addresses, the amount transferred, and a digital signature to verify the authenticity of the transaction.

3. **Blocks:** Transactions are grouped into blocks. These blocks are collections of data, typically containing a fixed number of transactions. For example, in the Bitcoin blockchain, a new block is added roughly every 10 minutes, containing a set of recent transactions. Each block also includes a reference to the previous block, forming a chain of blocks, hence the term "blockchain."

4. **Validation:** Before a block is added to the blockchain, it must be validated by the network's nodes. This process involves verifying the authenticity of each transaction, checking if the sender has sufficient funds, and ensuring that the transaction adheres to the network's rules (e.g., no double-spending). This validation process is known as consensus.

5. **Consensus Mechanisms**: Consensus mechanisms are the protocols that ensure that all nodes in the network agree on the validity of transactions and the order in which they are added to the blockchain. The most well-known consensus mechanism is Proof of Work (PoW), used by Bitcoin, where nodes compete to solve complex mathematical puzzles to add a new block. Other consensus mechanisms include Proof of Stake (PoS), Delegated Proof of Stake (DPoS), and more.

6. **Adding Blocks**: Once a block is validated, it is added to the blockchain, and all nodes on the network update their copies of the blockchain to include the new block. This process creates a chronological and immutable ledger of all transactions ever executed on the network.

7. **Security:** Blockchain technology relies on cryptographic techniques to secure transactions and data. Each block contains a cryptographic hash of the previous block, making it extremely difficult to alter any information in a block without changing all subsequent blocks, a task nearly impossible to achieve in a decentralized and widely distributed network.

8. **Transparency:** One of the key features of blockchain is transparency. All transactions are recorded on a public ledger, and anyone can view the entire transaction history. This transparency reduces the potential for fraud and builds trust in the system.

9. **Anonymity:** While transactions are transparent, the identities of the parties involved are typically represented by cryptographic addresses rather than real-world names. This provides a level of privacy and pseudonymity for users.

Cryptocurrency wallets and security:

Cryptocurrency Wallets:

A cryptocurrency wallet is a digital tool that allows you to store, send, and receive cryptocurrencies. These wallets come in various forms, each with its level of security and usability. Here are the main types of cryptocurrency wallets:

1. Software Wallets:

- **Desktop Wallets:** These are software applications installed on your computer. They offer good security if your computer is properly secured against malware and viruses.

- **Mobile Wallets**: Designed for smartphones, these apps are convenient for making on-the-go transactions. However, they may be less secure than desktop wallets if your mobile device is compromised.

- **Online/Web Wallets**: Web-based wallets are accessible through a browser. They are user-friendly but are considered less secure because they are vulnerable to hacking and phishing attacks.

2. Hardware Wallets:

- *Hardware wallets* are physical devices designed specifically for cryptocurrency storage. They are highly secure because they store your private keys offline, making them immune to online threats. Popular hardware wallet brands include Ledger and Trezor.

3. Paper Wallets:

- A paper wallet involves printing your cryptocurrency's public and private keys on a piece of paper. It's offline and secure from online attacks but can be easily damaged or lost.

4. Brain Wallets:

- A brain wallet is a wallet that generates keys based on a passphrase or a series of words chosen by the user. While they're easy to remember, they can be vulnerable to brute force attacks if the passphrase is weak.

Security Measures for Cryptocurrency Wallets:

Ensuring the security of your cryptocurrency wallet is paramount to protecting your assets from theft or loss. Here are some key security measures:

1. **Use Strong, Unique Passwords**:
   - Use a strong, complex password for your wallet and consider using a passphrase for extra security.

2. Enable Two-Factor Authentication (2FA):

- Whenever possible, enable 2FA for your wallet and any associated accounts. This adds an extra layer of security by requiring a one-time code from your mobile device or email.

3. Backup Your Wallet:

- Regularly back up your wallet's private keys or recovery phrases. Store these backups in a secure location, preferably offline. This ensures you can recover your funds if your wallet is lost or damaged.

4. Keep Software Up to Date:

- Ensure that the wallet software and your device's operating system are regularly updated to patch security vulnerabilities.

5. Beware of Phishing Attacks:

- Be cautious of emails or websites that ask for your wallet information or private keys. Always double-check the legitimacy of sources.

6. Consider Using Hardware Wallets:

- For significant holdings, consider investing in a hardware wallet, which provides the highest level of security.

7. Practice Cold Storage:

- Store a significant portion of your cryptocurrency holdings in cold storage (offline wallets like hardware wallets or paper wallets) to protect them from online threats.

8. **Educate Yourself:**

- Stay informed about the latest security practices and threats in the cryptocurrency space. Knowledge is your best defence against potential risks.

Remember that once your cryptocurrency is lost or stolen, it is often irreversible. Taking these security measures seriously can help safeguard your investments.

3

Market Fundamentals

Market orders vs. limit orders:

Market orders and limit orders are two common types of orders used in trading, including cryptocurrency trading on platforms like Binance. They serve different purposes and have distinct characteristics:

1. Market Order:

- **Definition**: A market order is an order to buy or sell an asset (such as a cryptocurrency) at the current market price. When you place a market order, you are essentially instructing the exchange to execute the order immediately at the best available price in the order book.

- **Execution**: Market orders are executed quickly because they prioritize speed over price. They guarantee that your order will be filled, but the exact price you receive may differ slightly from the current market price.

- **Use Cases**: Market orders are commonly used when traders want to enter or exit a position quickly and are less concerned about the exact price at which the trade is executed. They are suitable for highly liquid markets with narrow bid-ask spreads.

Example: If you place a market order to buy Bitcoin, you will buy it at the best available selling price at that moment, even if it's slightly higher than the last traded price.

2. Limit Order:

- **Definition**: A limit order is an order to buy or sell an asset at a specific price or better. Unlike market orders, limit orders allow you to specify the price at which you are willing to trade. The order will only be executed if the market reaches your specified price or a better one.

- **Execution**: Limit orders provide more control over the price at which your trade is executed, but they are not guaranteed to be filled immediately. Your order may remain in the order book until the market reaches your specified price or until it expires.

- **Use Cases**: Limit orders are preferred by traders who want to be more price-sensitive and patient. They are commonly used for setting entry and exit points, as well as profit-taking and stop-loss orders.

Example: If the current market price of Ethereum is $3,000, and you place a limit order to buy Ethereum at $2,900, your order will only be executed if the market price drops to or below $2,900.

Key Differences:

- Market orders prioritize speed of execution, while limit orders prioritize price control.

  - Market orders guarantee execution but not a specific price.

  - Limit orders offer price control but do not guarantee immediate execution.

  - Market orders are suitable for quick trades, while limit orders are useful for setting specific price levels.

Traders often use a combination of market and limit orders in their trading strategies, depending on their objectives and market conditions. Understanding when to use each order type is essential for effective trading and risk management.

Market depth and order book:

Market Depth:

Market depth, often referred to as "order book depth" or simply "depth," is a crucial concept in trading, including cryptocurrency trading. It provides traders with insights into the supply and demand dynamics of a particular cryptocurrency pair (e.g., BTC/USD or ETH/BTC) on an exchange. Understanding market depth is essential for making informed trading decisions.

Order Book:

The order book is a real-time, continuously updated list of buy and sell orders for a specific cryptocurrency pair on an exchange. It displays the orders from traders who want to buy the cryptocurrency at a specific price (bid orders) and those who want to sell it at a specific price (ask orders). The order book typically consists of two main components:

1. **Bid Orders (Buy Side)**: These are orders from traders who are willing to buy the cryptocurrency at a particular price. The highest bid order is usually at the top of the list, representing the highest price buyers are willing to pay. As you move down the list, the bid prices decrease.

2. Ask Orders (Sell Side): These are orders from traders who want to sell the cryptocurrency at a specific price. The lowest ask order is typically at the top, representing the lowest price at which sellers are willing to sell. As you move down the list, the ask prices increase.

Key Concepts and Usage:

Understanding market depth and the order book can be beneficial for traders in several ways:

1. **Price Discovery**: The order book helps traders determine the current market price for a cryptocurrency by showing the highest bid and lowest ask prices. The price at which these two meet is often referred to as the "market price" or "last traded price."

2. **Liquidity Assessment**: Traders can gauge the liquidity of a market by looking at the depth of the order book. A deep order book with many orders at various price levels usually indicates higher liquidity, making it easier to enter and exit positions without significant price fluctuations.

3. **Support and Resistance Levels**: Traders use the order book to identify support and resistance levels. For example, a strong cluster of buy orders at a specific price level may act as support, while a cluster of sell orders can act as resistance.

4. **Market Sentiment**: Changes in the order book, such as a sudden increase in buy orders, can indicate a bullish sentiment, while a surge in sell orders may suggest a bearish sentiment.

5. **Trading Strategies**: Some traders employ strategies like scalping or arbitrage based on the information gleaned from the order book.

6. **Risk Management**: By analyzing the order book, traders can anticipate potential price movements and set stop-loss and take-profit levels accordingly.

The order book and market depth are invaluable tools for cryptocurrency traders, offering insights into supply and demand dynamics, price levels, and market sentiment.

Candlestick charts and technical analysis:

Candlestick charts and technical analysis are essential tools for traders and investors in the financial markets, including cryptocurrency trading on platforms like Binance. They provide insights into price movements, trends, and potential future price movements. Here's a more detailed explanation of each:

Candlestick Charts:

Candlestick charts are a popular and visually informative way to represent price data for a given financial instrument, such as a cryptocurrency or stock. Each candlestick on the chart represents a specific period, which could be minutes, hours, days, weeks, or months, depending on the chosen timeframe. A single candlestick typically consists of four main components:

1. **Open Price (Open)**: The price at which the asset opened during the specified period.

2. **Close Price (Close)**: The price at which the asset closed at the end of the period.

3. **High Price (High)**: The highest price reached during the period.

4. **Low Price (Low):** The lowest price reached during the period.

The candlestick's body is defined by the open and closed prices, and the "wick" or "shadow" represents the high and low prices. Candlesticks come in various colours (often green for bullish candles and red for bearish candles) to indicate whether the closing price was higher or lower than the opening price.

Key candlestick patterns and signals include:

- **Bullish Engulfing**: When a small bearish candle is followed by a larger bullish candle, suggesting a potential reversal from a downtrend to an uptrend.

- **Bearish Engulfing**: The opposite of the bullish engulfing pattern, indicating a potential reversal from an uptrend to a downtrend.

- **Doji**: When the open and close prices are very close or the same, suggesting indecision in the market.

- **Hammer:** A candlestick with a small body and a long lower wick, often seen as a bullish reversal signal.

- **Shooting Star:** The opposite of the hammer, with a small body and a long upper wick, often seen as a bearish reversal signal.

Candlestick patterns are used in conjunction with other technical analysis tools to make trading decisions and predict future price movements.

Technical Analysis:

Technical analysis is a method of evaluating and predicting future price movements by analyzing historical price data and trading volume. It relies on the premise that historical price patterns tend to repeat themselves and that market psychology is reflected in price charts. Key concepts and tools in technical analysis include:

1. **Support and Resistance**: Identifying price levels at which an asset tends to find buying support (support) or selling pressure (resistance). These levels are crucial for making trading decisions.

2. **Trends**: Determining the direction of the market, whether it's in an uptrend (higher highs and higher lows), a downtrend (lower highs and lower lows), or a sideways trend (range-bound).

3. **Indicators:** Using technical indicators like moving averages, Relative Strength Index (RSI), and MACD to gain additional insights into market momentum, overbought or oversold conditions, and potential trend changes.

4. **Chart Patterns:** Recognizing patterns like head and shoulders, double tops, double bottoms, and flags that provide clues about future price movements.

5. **Fibonacci Retracement**: Applying Fibonacci levels to identify potential support and resistance levels based on the Fibonacci sequence, which is believed to have relevance in financial markets.

6. **Volume Analysis:** Examining trading volume to assess the strength of price movements and potential trend reversals.

Fundamental analysis in cryptocurrency trading:

Fundamental analysis in cryptocurrency trading involves evaluating the intrinsic value of a cryptocurrency by analyzing various factors and indicators that can influence its price and long-term potential. Unlike technical analysis, which primarily relies on historical price and volume data, fundamental analysis focuses on the underlying fundamentals of a cryptocurrency project. Here are key aspects and factors involved in the fundamental analysis of cryptocurrency trading:

1. **Project Team and Development**: Assess the development team behind the cryptocurrency project. Look for information about their experience, track record, and qualifications. A strong and reputable team is often seen as a positive sign.

2. **Whitepaper Analysis:** Read the project's whitepaper, which is a technical document that outlines the cryptocurrency's purpose, technology, use cases, and roadmap. Analyze whether the project has a clear and viable vision.

3. **Technology and Innovation:** Evaluate the underlying blockchain technology and the cryptocurrency's unique features. Consider factors like scalability, security, consensus mechanism, and any technological innovations the project brings to the table.

4. **Use Case and Utility:** Understand the real-world use case and utility of the cryptocurrency. Does it solve a genuine problem or address a specific need? A cryptocurrency with a practical use case may have more long-term potential.

5. **Market Demand and Adoption:** Analyze the demand for the cryptocurrency and its adoption in various industries or communities. High demand and growing adoption can positively impact the price.

6. **Competition**: Consider the competitive landscape within the cryptocurrency's niche. Are there similar projects with better features or a stronger community? Competitive analysis can help you gauge the project's potential relative to others.

7. **Partnerships and Alliances:** Investigate partnerships and alliances the project has formed with other companies, organizations, or blockchain projects. Strategic partnerships can enhance the project's credibility and adoption.

8. **Regulatory and Legal Factors**: Be aware of the regulatory environment surrounding cryptocurrency in different countries. Regulatory changes can have a significant impact on its value.

9. **Tokenomics**: Study the cryptocurrency's tokenomics, including its supply, distribution, and inflation rate. Factors like a limited supply (e.g., Bitcoin's 21 million cap) can influence long-term value.

10. **Community and Social Sentiment**: Monitor the cryptocurrency community on social media, forums, and news outlets. Positive sentiment and active engagement can contribute to price appreciation.

11. **Security and Vulnerabilities:** Investigate the security measures in place to protect the cryptocurrency from hacks and vulnerabilities. Security breaches can lead to a loss of trust and value.

12. **Economic and Macro Factors:** Consider broader economic and macroeconomic factors that can affect cryptocurrencies, such as inflation, interest rates, and geopolitical events.

13. **Adoption and Integration:** Pay attention to whether the cryptocurrency is being integrated into existing financial systems, platforms, or applications. Widespread adoption can lead to increased demand.

14. **Financial Metrics:** Analyze financial metrics if available, such as revenue, profit, or transaction volume, depending on the type of cryptocurrency. These metrics can provide insights into the project's financial   health.

4

Trading Strategies

Day trading, swing trading, and long-term investing:

1. Day Trading:

- **Definition:** Day trading involves buying and selling financial instruments, such as cryptocurrencies, within the same trading day. Day traders aim to profit from short-term price fluctuations.

- **Timeframe**: Day traders typically make multiple trades throughout a single day, with positions usually being closed before the market closes.

- **Strategy**: Day traders use technical analysis, charts, and real-time data to identify short-term price patterns and trends. They often rely on leverage (borrowed funds) to amplify potential gains, but this also increases the risk.

- **Risk**: Day trading can be highly volatile and stressful, as traders must make quick decisions and closely monitor the markets. It requires a deep understanding of technical analysis and the ability to manage risk effectively.

2. Swing Trading:

- **Definition:** Swing trading is a trading style that aims to capture shorter- to medium-term price movements within a broader trend. Swing traders hold positions for several days to weeks.

- **Timeframe**: Swing traders focus on intermediate price swings and trends, rather than short-term fluctuations or long-term investments.

- **Strategy**: Swing traders use technical and fundamental analysis to identify entry and exit points. They aim to ride the "swings" in the market, profiting from price movements in both upward and downward directions.

- **Risk:** While swing trading carries less stress than day trading, it still requires vigilance and risk management. Swing traders should be aware of market news and events that can impact their positions.

3. Long-Term Investing:

- **Definition:** Long-term investing, also known as "HODLing" in the cryptocurrency community (a play on the word "hold"), involves buying assets to hold them for an extended period, often years.

- **Timeframe**: Long-term investors are not concerned with short-term price fluctuations and are more interested in the potential for significant growth over time.

- **Strategy**: Long-term investors base their decisions on fundamental analysis, evaluating the underlying value and potential of the asset. They often have a buy-and-hold approach and may ignore short-term market noise.

- **Risk**: Long-term investing carries less day-to-day risk compared to day trading and swing trading, but investors are exposed to long-term market dynamics and events. Risk management is still important.

Choosing the right trading style depends on an individual's risk tolerance, time commitment, trading experience, and financial goals. Here are some key considerations:

- **Risk Tolerance**: Day trading is the riskiest, while long-term investing tends to be less risky. Assess your risk tolerance and choose a style that aligns with it.

- **Time Commitment**: Day trading requires constant monitoring, while long-term investing can be more passive. Swing trading falls in between in terms of time commitment.

- **Experience**: Novice traders may find long-term investing less daunting, as it requires less technical expertise compared to day trading. Experienced traders may explore swing trading or day trading.

- **Financial Goals:** Determine your financial goals. Day trading and swing trading are more suitable for those seeking short-term profits, while long-term investing is for those looking for sustained growth over time.

Risk management techniques:

Risk management is a crucial aspect of successful trading, and it involves strategies and practices aimed at protecting your capital and minimizing potential losses. Here are some risk management techniques commonly used by traders:

1. **Position Sizing**: Determine how much capital you are willing to risk on a single trade. A common rule of thumb is to risk no more than 1-2% of your total trading capital on any single trade. This ensures that you can withstand a series of losing trades without depleting your account.

2. **Stop-Loss Orders:** A stop-loss order is a predetermined price at which you will sell (or exit) a position to limit losses. Setting a stop-loss helps you define your risk in advance and ensures you don't let a losing trade turn into a catastrophe.

3. **Take-Profit Orders**: Similar to stop-loss orders, take-profit orders set a specific price at which you will sell to lock in profits. This helps you avoid the temptation to hold onto a winning trade for too long, potentially giving back gains.

4. **Risk-Reward Ratio**: Evaluate the potential reward against the risk for each trade. A common risk-reward ratio is 1:2, which means that for every dollar you risk (your stop-loss), you aim to make at

least two dollars in profit. This ensures that your winning trades can offset losses over time.

5. **Diversification**: Don't put all your capital into a single asset or trade. Diversify your portfolio to spread risk. Even within the cryptocurrency market, consider trading different coins or tokens rather than going all-in on one.

6. **Position Diversification:** Even within a single trade, consider breaking your position into smaller parts and scaling in gradually. This can help you manage risk if the market moves against you initially.

7. **Use Leverage Wisely**: If you engage in margin trading or derivatives, be cautious with leverage. High leverage can amplify both gains and losses. Only use leverage if you fully understand its implications and can manage the increased risk.

8. **Risk Tolerance Assessment**: Assess your personal risk tolerance and only take positions that align with your risk tolerance. If you're uncomfortable with significant fluctuations, consider more conservative assets or strategies.

9. **Continuous Learning:** Stay informed about the assets you're trading, market conditions, and global news that might affect prices. The more you know, the better you can make informed decisions.

10. **Emotional Control:** Keep emotions like fear and greed in check. Emotional trading often leads to impulsive decisions and larger losses. Stick to your trading plan and strategy, even in volatile markets.

11. **Portfolio Rebalancing**: Regularly review and adjust your portfolio to maintain your desired risk exposure. If certain assets have performed well and become a significant portion of your portfolio, consider rebalancing to reduce risk.

12. **Backtesting and Analysis:** Before implementing a trading strategy, backtest it using historical data to assess its performance and risk profile. Adjust the strategy as needed based on the results.

13. **Paper Trading:** If you're new to trading or testing a new strategy, consider "paper" or demo trading without real money to practice and refine your approach without risking capital.

Remember that no risk management technique can guarantee profits or prevent all losses. The goal is to create a disciplined and systematic approach to trading that reduces the impact of potential losses on your overall capital.

Setting up a trading plan:

Setting up a trading plan is a critical step for any trader, whether you're a beginner or an experienced professional. A well-thought-out trading plan can help you navigate the volatile world of trading, manage risk, and improve your chances of success. Here's a more detailed explanation of the key components of setting up a trading plan:

1. Define Your Goals and Objectives:

- Start by clearly defining your trading goals. Are you looking to generate income, build long-term wealth, or simply learn more about the markets?

  - Set specific, measurable, achievable, relevant, and time-bound (SMART) goals. For example, "I want to achieve a 10% return on my trading capital within six months."

2. Risk Tolerance and Capital Allocation:

- Determine how much capital you're willing to risk in your trading activities. This is often referred to as your risk capital.

  - Establish your risk tolerance level. Are you comfortable with high-risk, high-reward strategies, or do you prefer a more conservative approach?

  - Decide what portion of your overall portfolio you'll allocate to trading. It's generally advisable to avoid risking more than a small percentage of your total capital on a single trade.

3. Trading Strategy:

- Select a trading strategy that aligns with your goals and risk tolerance. Common strategies include day trading, swing trading, trend following, and value investing.

- Detail your chosen strategy, including entry and exit criteria, technical indicators, and fundamental factors you'll consider.

4. Position Sizing and Risk Management:

- Determine how much of your capital you'll risk on each trade (position sizing). This is often expressed as a percentage of your risk capital.

- Implement stop-loss orders to limit potential losses on each trade. Your stop-loss should be based on your risk tolerance and the specific trade setup.

- Consider setting a maximum daily or weekly loss limit to prevent emotional decision-making during losing streaks.

5. Trade Management:

- Outline how you'll manage open trades. This includes setting profit targets and trailing stops.

- Decide if you'll actively monitor your positions or use a more passive approach.

6. Record Keeping and Analysis:

- Keep a detailed trading journal to track all your trades, including entry and exit prices, trade size, reasons for entering the trade, and outcomes.

    - Regularly review and analyze your trading journal to identify patterns, strengths, and weaknesses in your trading strategy.

7. Emotional Discipline:

- Develop a plan for managing emotions, such as fear and greed, which can lead to impulsive decisions.

    - Stick to your trading plan and avoid deviating from it based on emotional reactions.

8. Continuous Learning and Adaptation:

- Recognize that the markets evolve, and your trading plan should too. Be open to adjusting your strategies and rules based on changing market conditions.

9. Backtesting and Simulation:

- Before implementing your trading plan with real money, consider backtesting it on historical data to evaluate its performance.

    - You can also use paper trading or simulation accounts to practice your strategy without risking actual capital.

10. Contingency Planning:

- Have a plan for what you'll do in case of unexpected events, market disruptions, or technical issues with your trading platform.

Psychological aspects of trading:

Psychological aspects of trading are critically important and often overlooked by many traders, especially those who are just starting. Successful trading is not just about analyzing charts and making informed decisions; it also involves understanding and managing your own emotions and behaviour. Here are some key psychological aspects of trading:

1. Emotional Control:

- **Greed**: One common pitfall is becoming too greedy when a trade is going well, leading to overconfidence and risky decisions.
  - **Fear**: Conversely, fear can cause traders to panic and sell too early when a trade is in the red, missing out on potential profits.

2. Discipline:

- **Sticking to a Trading Plan**: Having a well-defined trading plan is essential. Discipline involves following your plan even when emotions are urging you to deviate.

   - **Avoiding Impulsive Actions:** Impulsive decisions often lead to losses. Discipline is about controlling the urge to make hasty trades.

3. Risk Management:

- **Position Sizing:** Traders need to determine how much capital to risk on each trade. Avoiding over-leveraging and risking too much on a single trade is crucial.

   - **Stop-Loss and Take-Profit Orders**: Setting stop-loss and take-profit orders can help limit losses and lock in profits.

4. Patience:

- **Waiting for Opportunities**: Successful traders often spend a significant amount of time waiting for the right trading opportunities to arise, rather than forcing trades when the market isn't favourable.

   - **Long-Term Perspective**: Patience also involves not being overly concerned with short-term fluctuations and maintaining a long-term perspective.

5. Stress Management:

- Trading can be stressful, especially during volatile market conditions. It's important to have healthy coping mechanisms to deal with stress, such as exercise, meditation, or taking breaks from trading.

6. Continuous Learning:

- The ability to adapt and learn from both successful and unsuccessful trades is crucial. Being open to new strategies and adjusting your approach as the market evolves is a sign of a resilient trader.

7. Overcoming Biases:

- Cognitive biases, such as confirmation bias (seeking information that confirms your beliefs) or loss aversion (the tendency to prefer avoiding losses over achieving equivalent gains), can cloud judgment. Being aware of these biases is the first step in overcoming them.

8. Keeping Emotions in Check:

- Trading can be an emotional rollercoaster. It's important to recognize when emotions are influencing your decisions and take steps to regain rationality.

9. Record-Keeping:

- Maintaining a trading journal can help you track your trades, strategies, and emotions. It allows you to review your performance objectively and make improvements.

10. Seeking Support:

- Many traders find it helpful to have a support network or a mentor. Discussing trading strategies and experiences with others can provide valuable insights and emotional support.

5

Deposits and Withdrawals

How to deposit funds on Binance:

Depositing funds on Binance is a fundamental step to start trading or investing in cryptocurrencies on the platform. Here's a detailed explanation of how to deposit funds on Binance:

1. Sign in to Your Binance Account:

- Go to the official Binance website *(https://www.binance.com/)*.

   - Log in to your Binance account using your registered email address and password.

2. Access the Deposit Page:

- After logging in, hover your mouse over the "Funds" tab in the top menu and click on "Deposit."

3. Select the Cryptocurrency to Deposit:

- On the deposit page, you'll see a list of cryptocurrencies supported by Binance. Choose the cryptocurrency you want to deposit. Ensure that you are selecting the correct coin/token, as sending the wrong cryptocurrency to your Binance wallet can result in the loss of funds.

4. Generate a Deposit Address:

- Once you've selected the cryptocurrency you want to deposit, Binance will generate a deposit address for that specific coin/token. This address is a long alphanumeric string unique to your Binance account. It's where you'll send your funds from your external wallet or exchange.

5. Copy the Deposit Address:

- Click on the "Copy Address" button next to the generated deposit address. Make sure you copy the entire address accurately.

6. Transfer Funds to Binance:

- Open your external cryptocurrency wallet or the account from which you want to send funds to Binance.

    - Initiate a transfer or withdrawal from your external wallet or exchange platform.

    - Paste the Binance deposit address you copied in step 5 as the recipient address.

- Double-check the address to ensure it's correct. Sending the wrong cryptocurrency to the address can result in the loss of your funds.

7. Confirm the Transaction:

- Depending on your external wallet or exchange, you may need to enter the amount you want to transfer and possibly other information.

- Confirm the transaction, and make sure to review any fees associated with the transfer.

8. Wait for Confirmation:

- Once you initiate the transfer, you'll need to wait for confirmations on the blockchain. The time it takes for confirmations varies depending on the cryptocurrency you're depositing and network congestion. You can check the transaction status on the blockchain explorer.

9. Funds in Your Binance Wallet:

- After the transaction is confirmed, the funds will appear in your Binance account. You can check your Binance wallet's balance under the "Funds" tab.

Please be aware of the following important points:

- Always double-check the deposit address to ensure accuracy.

   - Some cryptocurrencies may have a minimum deposit requirement, so make sure you meet that threshold.

   - Binance may have specific rules and fees associated with certain deposits, so review these before making a deposit.

   - If you're depositing a cryptocurrency that isn't natively supported by Binance, you may need to use the Binance Smart Chain (BSC) or convert it to a supported asset within Binance.

Withdrawal options and fees:

Withdrawal Options:

1. **Cryptocurrency Withdrawals:** Binance allows users to withdraw their funds in various cryptocurrencies. This section would explain how to initiate a cryptocurrency withdrawal, including selecting the cryptocurrency you want to withdraw, providing the destination address (external wallet or exchange), and specifying the amount to withdraw.

2. **Fiat Currency Withdrawals**: Some regions and users have access to fiat currency withdrawals on Binance. This might involve withdrawing funds in your local currency to your linked bank account. The process and options for fiat withdrawals would be explained in this section.

3. **Binance Card**: If applicable, information on using the Binance Card for withdrawals would be covered. The Binance Card is a cryptocurrency debit card that allows users to spend their crypto holdings at merchants that accept Visa.

4. **P2P Trading for Withdrawals**: Binance's Peer-to-Peer (P2P) trading platform allows users to buy and sell cryptocurrencies with other users using various payment methods. This section could detail how to use P2P trading to facilitate withdrawals.

Withdrawal Fees:

1. **Network Transaction Fees:** Every cryptocurrency withdrawal typically incurs a network transaction fee. This fee goes to miners or validators on the blockchain network and varies based on network congestion and the specific cryptocurrency being withdrawn.

2. **Binance Withdrawal Fees:** Binance itself may charge withdrawal fees on top of the network transaction fees. These fees

can vary depending on the cryptocurrency and are used to cover administrative and operational costs.

3. **Discounts and BNB:** Users might learn how to reduce withdrawal fees by using Binance Coin (BNB) to pay for transaction fees. Binance often offers fee discounts for BNB holders.

4. **VIP Level and Fee Discounts**: Binance offers different VIP levels based on trading volume. Users with higher VIP levels may be eligible for lower withdrawal fees. This section would explain how VIP levels work and how to achieve them.

Withdrawing Safely:

1. **Security Measures:** The chapter might emphasize the importance of security when making withdrawals, including enabling two-factor authentication (2FA), whitelisting withdrawal addresses, and monitoring account activity.

2. **Double-Checking Withdrawal Details:** Stress the need for double-checking withdrawal details, such as the recipient's address, to avoid sending funds to the wrong destination.

3. **Withdrawal Limits:** Explain any withdrawal limits or restrictions based on verification levels and how to increase these limits.

4. **Customer Support:** Provide guidance on what to do in case of withdrawal issues or delays and how to contact Binance's customer support.

Security measures for your Binance account:

Security measures for your Binance account are crucial to protect your assets and personal information in the world of cryptocurrency trading, where the risk of hacking and fraud is ever-present. Binance offers several security features and practices to help safeguard your account. Here are some important security measures you should consider when using Binance:

1. Two-Factor Authentication (2FA):

- Enable 2FA on your Binance account. This adds an extra layer of security by requiring you to enter a one-time code from a mobile app like Google Authenticator or receive it via SMS whenever you log in or make withdrawals.

2. Email Verification:

- Verify your email address associated with your Binance account. This helps in account recovery and security notifications.

3. Withdrawal Whitelists:

- Set up withdrawal whitelists, which allow you to specify a list of wallet addresses that you trust for withdrawals. Any withdrawal to an address not on the whitelist will be blocked.

4. Anti-Phishing Code:

- Create an anti-phishing code in your account settings. This code helps you verify the authenticity of Binance emails and communications to protect against phishing attempts.

5. Strong Password:

- Use a strong, unique password for your Binance account. Avoid using easily guessable passwords and consider using a password manager.

6. Secure Your Email:

- Ensure that your email account (the one linked to Binance) is also secure. Use a strong password and enable 2FA if your email provider offers it.

7. Account Activity Monitoring:

- Regularly review your account activity and transactions for any suspicious activity. Binance provides a history of login and withdrawal attempts that you can check.

8. Device Security:

- Only use trusted and secure devices to access your Binance account. Avoid using public computers or unsecured networks for logging in.

9. Binance API Management:

- If you use API keys for trading bots or applications, manage them carefully. Only provide necessary permissions and revoke access for any unused or suspicious keys.

10. Trust Wallet:

- If you use Binance's Trust Wallet, ensure you set up its security features, like biometric authentication or PIN codes.

11. Binance Security Center:

- Regularly visit Binance's Security Center, which provides educational resources and recommendations for enhancing your account security.

12. Multi-Account Login Alerts:

- Enable alerts for multi-account logins. Binance will notify you if your account is accessed from a different device or location.

13. Backup and Recovery:

- Keep a secure backup of your 2FA codes and other account recovery information in a safe place. Consider writing down backup codes and storing them offline.

14. Customer Support Vigilance:

- Be cautious of unsolicited communication from "Binance support." Binance will not ask for your password or 2FA codes via email or other means.

15. Education:

- Continuously educate yourself about the latest security threats and best practices in cryptocurrency security.

6

Trading on Binance

Navigating the Binance trading platform:

Navigating the Binance trading platform is crucial for anyone looking to engage in cryptocurrency trading on this exchange. Binance provides a user-friendly interface with a wide range of features and tools to assist traders. Here's a more detailed explanation of how to navigate the Binance trading platform:

1. Login and Dashboard:

- Begin by logging into your Binance account.

- Once logged in, you'll be directed to your dashboard, which is the main hub for accessing various features.

2. Selecting a Trading Pair:

- Binance offers a vast selection of cryptocurrency trading pairs. You can typically find them on the trading dashboard.

- A trading pair consists of two cryptocurrencies, such as BTC/USD or ETH/BTC. You need to choose a pair to trade.

3. Basic Trading View:

- Binance provides two main trading views: Basic and Advanced. Start with the Basic view if you're new to trading.

- In the Basic view, you'll see the price chart for your selected trading pair, order book, and recent trade history.

4. Price Chart:

- The price chart displays the historical price movements of the selected cryptocurrency pair.

- You can customize the chart by adjusting the timeframes (e.g., 1-hour, 4-hour, 1-day) and using technical analysis tools like trendlines, indicators, and drawing tools.

5. Order Book:

- The order book shows all the buy and sell orders for the selected pair.

- The buy orders are typically on the left side, and the sell orders are on the right. The middle price is the current market price.

6. Placing Orders:

- Below the price chart and order book, you can place different types of orders: market, limit, and stop-limit orders.

    - Market orders execute immediately at the current market price.

    - Limit orders allow you to set a specific price at which you want your order to execute.

    - Stop-limit orders combine stop and limit prices and are used to trigger orders when the market reaches a certain price.

7. Trade History:

- The trade history section displays recent trades for the selected trading pair, including the price, quantity, and time of execution.

8. Account Information:

- Your account balance and available funds are usually displayed on the right side of the dashboard.

    - You can also access your trading history, open orders, and other account-related information from this section.

9. Additional Features:

- Binance's trading platform may include additional features like a margin trading section, futures trading, staking options, and more.

    - Explore these features if you're interested in advanced trading strategies.

10. Security and Settings:

- You can access your account settings and security features from the user profile menu.

    - Ensure your account is properly secured with two-factor authentication (2FA) and review security settings regularly.

11. Mobile Trading App:

- Binance offers a mobile trading app for trading on the go. It provides a similar interface and functionality to the web platform.

12. Help and Support:

- If you have questions or encounter issues while navigating the platform, Binance offers customer support and a help center to assist users.

Placing orders on Binance:

Placing orders on Binance is a fundamental aspect of cryptocurrency trading. Binance offers several types of orders that traders can use to buy or sell cryptocurrencies on its platform. Each type of order serves a different purpose and allows traders to execute their trading strategies efficiently. Here's an explanation of some common order types on Binance:

1. **Market Order:** A market order is the simplest type of order. When you place a market order, you are instructing Binance to buy or sell a cryptocurrency at the current market price. Market orders are executed quickly, but the exact price at which the order is filled may vary slightly from the current market price due to price fluctuations. Market orders are suitable for traders who want to execute a trade immediately and are less concerned about the exact price.

2. **Limit Order:** A limit order allows you to specify the exact price at which you want to buy or sell a cryptocurrency. If you place a buy limit order, it will only be executed when the market price reaches or goes below your specified price. If you place a sell limit order, it will only be executed when the market price reaches or goes above your specified price. Limit orders give you more control over the execution price but may not be filled if the market doesn't reach your chosen price.

3. **Stop-Limit Order:** A stop-limit order is a combination of a stop order and a limit order. It involves setting two prices: the stop price and the limit price. When the market reaches the stop price, a limit order is placed at the limit price. If the market moves against you, a stop-limit order can help you limit your losses.

4. **Stop-Market Order:** Similar to the stop-limit order, a stop-market order involves setting a stop price. However, when the stop price is reached, a market order is executed rather than a limit order. This means that the order will be filled at the best available market price once the stop price is triggered.

5. **OCO (One Cancels the Other) Order**: An OCO order allows you to place two orders simultaneously: a take-profit order and a stop-loss order. If one of these orders is executed, the other is automatically canceled. It's a risk management tool that helps traders lock in profits or limit losses.

6. **Trailing Stop Order:** A trailing stop order is a dynamic stop-loss order that adjusts based on the cryptocurrency's price movement. You set a trailing percentage or fixed amount, and the stop price follows the market price at a set distance. If the market moves in your favor, the stop price moves with it, helping you secure gains. If the market reverses, the stop price remains fixed until it's hit.

7. **Iceberg Order:** An iceberg order allows you to place a large order that's hidden from the order book. Only a portion of the order is visible, protecting your trading intentions from other traders. As

the visible portion gets executed, more of the order becomes visible until the entire order is filled.

When placing orders on Binance, it's essential to consider your trading strategy, risk tolerance, and market conditions. The choice of order type depends on your specific goals, whether you want to execute quickly, set specific price levels, or implement risk management strategies. It's also crucial to double-check the details of your order before confirming, as errors can lead to unexpected outcomes in your trades.

Using advanced trading features:

1. **Margin Trading:** Margin trading allows traders to borrow funds to increase their trading positions beyond what they can afford with their own capital. This section would explain how margin trading works on Binance, including how to leverage your trades, manage risk with stop-loss orders, and calculate liquidation prices.

2. **Derivatives and Perpetual Contracts**: Binance offers derivative products such as futures and perpetual contracts. This part of the chapter would introduce these products, explain how they differ from spot trading, and provide guidance on how to trade them

effectively. Topics might include contract specifications, leverage, and managing positions.

3. **Leveraged Tokens**: Binance has introduced leveraged tokens that simplify the process of trading with leverage. This section would explore how these tokens work, their advantages, and how to use them as part of your trading strategy.

4. **Staking and Savings**: Binance allows users to stake certain cryptocurrencies and earn rewards or interest. This part of the chapter would cover the benefits of staking, how to participate in staking programs, and how to use the Binance Savings platform to earn interest on your holdings.

5. **Binance Trading Bots**: Discuss the use of trading bots on Binance. Explain what trading bots are, how they work, and the advantages and risks associated with automated trading. Provide information on using third-party trading bot platforms or Binance's own trading bot features.

6. **Advanced Charting Tools**: Explore Binance's advanced charting tools and indicators for technical analysis. This could include tutorials on using tools like Moving Averages, Relative Strength Index (RSI), MACD, and Fibonacci retracement levels. Provide examples of how to perform technical analysis and make informed trading decisions.

7. **Hedging Strategies**: Discuss hedging strategies to protect your portfolio from adverse market movements. Explain how to use options or other derivatives to hedge against potential losses.

8. **Risk Management for Advanced Traders**: Dive deeper into risk management techniques for advanced traders, including position sizing, portfolio diversification, and using stop-limit orders effectively.

9. **Liquidity Pools and Yield Farming**: Cover the concept of liquidity pools and yield farming in decentralized finance (DeFi). Explain how to provide liquidity to earn rewards and how to assess the risks associated with these activities.

10. **Cryptocurrency Taxation:** Discuss the tax implications of advanced trading strategies, such as margin trading and derivatives. Explain how to keep track of your trading activity for tax reporting purposes.

Tips for efficient trading on Binance:

1. **Educate Yourself:** Before you start trading, take the time to educate yourself about cryptocurrency markets, trading

strategies, and technical analysis. Understanding the assets you're trading and the market dynamics is crucial.

2. **Start with a Trading Plan**: Develop a clear trading plan that includes your goals, risk tolerance, and strategies. Decide on the type of trading you want to engage in, such as day trading, swing trading, or long-term investing.

3. **Risk Management:** Never risk more than you can afford to lose. Use risk management tools like stop-loss and take-profit orders to limit potential losses. Diversify your portfolio to spread risk across different assets.

4. **Use Technical Analysis**: Learn to read and analyze price charts and use technical indicators like Moving Averages, Relative Strength Index (RSI), and Bollinger Bands to make informed trading decisions.

5. **Stay Informed:** Keep up with the latest news and developments in the cryptocurrency space. Market sentiment can be heavily influenced by news, regulatory changes, and technological advancements.

6. **Practice on a Demo Account**: Binance offers a demo trading feature that allows you to practice without risking real money. Use this to familiarize yourself with the platform and test your strategies.

7. **Set Realistic Goals**: Don't expect to get rich overnight. Set realistic, achievable goals for your trading activities, and be patient. Successful trading often involves small, consistent gains over time.

8. **Avoid Emotional Trading**: Emotional trading, driven by fear and greed, can lead to impulsive decisions and losses.

Stick to your trading plan and avoid making decisions based on emotions.

9. **Leverage Wisely**: If you decide to use leverage for margin trading, do so with caution. High leverage can amplify both gains and losses. Understand how leverage works and its associated risks.

10. **Keep Records:** Maintain a detailed trading journal to track your trades, strategies, and results. This will help you analyze your performance and make improvements over time.

11. **Stay Secure:** Ensure the security of your Binance account by using strong passwords, enabling two-factor authentication (2FA), and being cautious of phishing attempts and scams.

12. **Understand Fees:** Familiarize yourself with Binance's fee structure. Different types of orders and trading pairs may have different fee rates. Understand how fees can impact your profits.

13. **Stay Disciplined**: Discipline is key to successful trading. Stick to your trading plan, avoid overtrading, and don't chase losses by making impulsive trades.

14. **Continuous Learning**: The cryptocurrency market is dynamic and constantly evolving. Stay open to learning and adapting your strategies as market conditions change.

7

Altcoins and Tokens

Exploring different altcoins and tokens:

Exploring different altcoins and tokens is a crucial aspect of cryptocurrency trading and investment. Altcoins and tokens are digital assets that exist on blockchain networks other than Bitcoin's. They offer various use cases and can belong to different categories based on their functions and characteristics. Here's an explanation of exploring altcoins and tokens with their categories:

1. Payment Coins:

- **Bitcoin (BTC)** is the original cryptocurrency and primarily functions as a decentralized digital currency for peer-to-peer transactions.

- **Litecoin (LTC), Bitcoin Cash (BCH),** and **Dash (DASH)** are examples of altcoins that also serve as digital currencies for payments.

2. Smart Contract Platforms:

- **Ethereum (ETH)** is the leading platform for creating and executing smart contracts, which are self-executing contracts with the terms of the agreement directly written into code.

    - **Cardano (ADA), Polkadot (DOT),** and **Solana (SOL)** are examples of platforms that compete with Ethereum, offering smart contract capabilities and scalability.

3. Privacy Coins:

- **Monero (XMR)** and **Zcash (ZEC)** are cryptocurrencies designed to provide enhanced privacy and anonymity for users' transactions.

    - These coins use advanced cryptographic techniques to obscure transaction details.

4. Stablecoins:

- **Tether (USDT), USDC (USD Coin),** and **DAI** are examples of stablecoins, which are digital assets pegged to the value of fiat currencies like the US dollar.

    - They provide stability in price and are often used as a store of value or for transferring funds between exchanges.

5. Utility Tokens:

- Tokens like **Binance Coin (BNB) and Ethereum's Ether (ETH)** are utility tokens used within their respective blockchain ecosystems.
    - They can be used to pay for transaction fees, access decentralized applications (dApps), or participate in governance.

6. Security Tokens:

- Security tokens represent ownership in a real-world asset, such as equity in a company, real estate, or other financial instruments.
    - They are regulated and offer investors a share in the underlying asset's value.

7. Non-Fungible Tokens (NFTs):

- NFTs are unique digital assets that represent ownership of a specific item, artwork, collectible, or in-game asset.
    - Examples include **CryptoKitties,** digital art NFTs, and in-game items like **Axie Infinity (AXS).**

8. DeFi Tokens:

- DeFi (Decentralized Finance) tokens are used within decentralized finance protocols and platforms.
    - Examples include **Uniswap (UNI)** for decentralized exchanges, **Compound (COMP)** for lending, and **Aave (AAVE)** for borrowing and lending.

9. Gaming Tokens:

- Gaming tokens are used in the gaming industry for in-game purchases, rewards, and digital asset ownership.
    - Examples include **Enjin Coin (ENJ)** and **Decentraland (MANA).**

10. Interoperability Tokens:

- These tokens aim to bridge different blockchain networks, enabling seamless communication and asset transfers.
    - Examples include **Chainlink (LINK) and Cosmos (ATOM).**

How to research and evaluate new coins:

Researching and evaluating new coins in the cryptocurrency market is crucial to make informed investment decisions and avoid potential scams or poor investments. Here is a step-by-step guide on how to research and evaluate new coins:

1. Understand the Basics of the Coin:

- Start by reading the whitepaper or project documentation. This document provides detailed information about the coin's purpose, technology, team, and roadmap. Look for clarity, transparency, and the uniqueness of the project.

2. Explore the Team:

- Research the team behind the coin. Look for information about their experience, qualifications, and past achievements. An experienced and credible team is more likely to execute the project successfully.

3. Check the Community and Social Media Presence:

- Join the coin's official social media channels, such as Telegram, Twitter, Reddit, and Discord. Analyze the level of community engagement and the quality of discussions. A strong and active community can indicate a healthy project.

4. Assess the Use Case:

- Determine the real-world problem the coin aims to solve. Evaluate whether the use case is practical, relevant, and has a market demand. Coins with a clear and practical use case are more likely to succeed.

5. Market Capitalization and Volume:

- Check the coin's market capitalization and trading volume on reputable cryptocurrency exchanges. Higher market cap and trading volume often indicate liquidity and investor interest.

6. Technology and Development:

- Investigate the technology behind the coin. Is it based on a secure and well-established blockchain? Are there regular updates and development activity on the code repository (e.g., GitHub)? A strong and active development team is essential.

7. Partnerships and Alliances:

- Look for partnerships and alliances the project has established. Partnerships with reputable companies or organizations can add credibility to the project.

8. Tokenomics and Supply:

- Understand the coin's tokenomics, including its total supply, circulating supply, and distribution. High token concentration among a few holders may pose risks to the coin's stability.

9. Roadmap and Milestones:

- Analyze the project's roadmap to see what milestones it has achieved and its future plans. A clear and achievable roadmap can indicate a well-thought-out project.

10. Security and Audits:

- Check if the coin has undergone security audits by reputable firms. Audited coins are generally considered safer investments.

11. Market Sentiment:

- Gauge market sentiment and opinions by reading news articles, blogs, and reviews from reputable cryptocurrency news sources and influencers.

12. Risks and Concerns:

- Identify potential risks and concerns associated with the coin or project. Consider factors such as regulatory issues, competition, and technology vulnerabilities.

13. Seek Expert Opinions:

- Consult cryptocurrency experts and forums for their opinions on the coin. Forums like Bitcointalk and Reddit can provide valuable insights and user experiences.

14. Create a Diversified Portfolio:

- Don't put all your funds into a single new coin. Diversify your cryptocurrency portfolio to spread risk.

15. Stay Informed:

- Continue to monitor the coin's progress and the broader cryptocurrency market. Market conditions can change rapidly, and ongoing research is essential.

Remember that investing in cryptocurrencies carries inherent risks, and there are no guarantees of profit. It's essential to conduct thorough research and due diligence before making any investment decisions.

Diversifying your portfolio:

Diversifying your portfolio is a fundamental strategy in investment and trading, including in the context of cryptocurrency trading on platforms like Binance. It involves spreading your investments across a range of different assets, asset classes, or trading strategies to reduce risk and potentially enhance returns. Here's an explanation of why diversification is important and how to implement it:

Importance of Diversification:

1. **Risk Mitigation:** Diversification helps reduce the impact of a poor-performing asset on your overall portfolio. If you put all your funds into a single cryptocurrency and it crashes in value, you could incur substantial losses. Diversifying across multiple assets can help mitigate such risks.

2. **Enhanced Stability:** Diversification can lead to a more stable portfolio since different assets often have different price movements. When one asset performs poorly, another might perform well, helping to balance out overall returns.

3. **Capital Preservation**: By spreading your investments, you can protect your capital. Even if one part of your portfolio experiences losses, gains in other areas can help offset those losses.

4. **Potential for Better Returns**: While diversification is primarily about risk reduction, it can also potentially lead to better overall

returns. A well-diversified portfolio can capture gains from various market sectors or assets that are performing well.

How to Diversify Your Cryptocurrency Portfolio on Binance:

1. **Choose Different Cryptocurrencies:** Invest in a variety of cryptocurrencies rather than concentrating all your funds in a single coin. Research and select assets with different use cases, market capitalizations, and development teams. Examples include Bitcoin (BTC), Ethereum (ETH), and various altcoins.

2. **Allocate Across Asset Classes:** Beyond cryptocurrencies, consider diversifying into other asset classes such as stablecoins, fiat currencies, or even traditional investments like stocks or bonds if your exchange offers such options.

3. **Geographic Diversification:** Cryptocurrency markets can vary significantly by region. Explore assets from different geographic areas to minimize exposure to region-specific risks.

4. **Use Different Investment Strategies:** If Binance offers different trading options, explore them. For example, you can engage in spot trading, margin trading, or even yield farming. Each strategy comes with its own risk profile, and diversifying your trading strategies can be as important as diversifying assets.

5. **Rebalance Regularly**: As market conditions change, the composition of your portfolio can drift from your original diversification goals. Periodically rebalance your portfolio by selling some of the assets that have appreciated significantly and reallocating those funds into assets that may have underperformed.

6. **Risk Assessment**: While diversification is important, it's also crucial to assess the risk associated with each asset or strategy you're considering. Some assets may have unique risks, so conduct thorough research and understand the potential downsides.

7. **Stay Informed**: Keep up with cryptocurrency news, market trends, and regulatory developments. Staying informed will help you make informed decisions about when and how to diversify your portfolio.

8

Binance Features and Services

Binance Futures and Options Trading:

Binance offers Futures and Options trading as advanced derivatives products for cryptocurrency traders. These products allow traders to speculate on the future price movements of cryptocurrencies without actually owning the underlying assets. Here's an explanation of Binance Futures and Options trading:

1. Binance Futures Trading:

Binance Futures is a platform that allows traders to engage in futures contracts trading for various cryptocurrencies. Futures contracts are financial derivatives that obligate the buyer to purchase, and the seller to sell, a specific amount of an underlying asset (in this case, a cryptocurrency) at a predetermined price and date in the future.

Key features of Binance Futures:

- **Leverage**: Traders can use leverage to amplify their positions, potentially leading to higher profits or losses. Binance offers different levels of leverage for various trading pairs, which can be adjusted by the trader.

- **Long and Short Positions**: Traders can take both long (buy) and short (sell) positions on futures contracts. This means they can profit from both rising and falling cryptocurrency prices.

- **Variety of Contracts:** Binance offers various types of futures contracts, including perpetual contracts (no expiration), quarterly futures, and more, covering a wide range of cryptocurrencies.

- **Risk Management**: Traders can set stop-loss and take-profit orders to manage risk and protect their investments.

- **Advanced Trading Tools:** Binance provides traders with advanced trading tools and charts to conduct technical and fundamental analysis.

- **Liquidation**: To manage risk and prevent account balances from going negative due to excessive losses, Binance employs a liquidation system that automatically closes positions if they reach a certain loss threshold.

2. Binance Options Trading:

Binance Options is another derivatives product that allows traders to buy and sell options contracts based on cryptocurrencies. Options give traders the right (but not the obligation) to buy (call option) or sell (put option) a specific cryptocurrency at a predetermined price (strike price) on or before a specific date (expiration date).

Key features of Binance Options:

- **Call and Put Options**: Traders can buy call options if they believe the price of the underlying cryptocurrency will rise, and put options if they expect it to fall.

- **Strike Prices and Expiry Dates**: Options contracts have strike prices and expiration dates, allowing traders to choose from various contract options to match their market outlook.

- **Limited Risk**: When buying options, traders have limited risk to the premium they pay for the option. They cannot lose more than the premium.

- **Flexibility**: Binance Options provide flexibility in terms of choosing different strike prices and expiration dates to tailor positions to specific market expectations.

- **Advanced Trading Strategies:** Traders can use options to implement complex trading strategies, such as straddles, strangles, and spreads, for hedging or speculation.

Binance Staking and Savings:

Binance Staking and Savings are two separate but related features offered by the Binance cryptocurrency exchange platform that allow users to earn rewards or interest on their cryptocurrencies. Here's a detailed explanation of each:

Binance Staking:

Binance Staking allows users to lock up or "stake" their cryptocurrencies to support the operations of various blockchain networks and, in return, earn staking rewards. Staking is primarily associated with Proof of Stake (PoS) or Delegated Proof of Stake (DPoS) blockchain networks. Here's how it works:

1. **Selecting a Supported Asset:** Binance typically offers staking support for specific cryptocurrencies or tokens that operate on PoS or DPoS blockchains. These assets may include popular coins like Tezos (XTZ), Polkadot (DOT), Cardano (ADA), and many others.

2. **Staking Your Assets**: To participate, users need to hold a certain amount of the supported cryptocurrency in their Binance account. They can then opt to stake these assets by following the staking instructions provided on the Binance platform.

3. **Earning Rewards**: By staking their assets, users contribute to the security and operation of the respective blockchain network. In return, they receive staking rewards, which are usually paid out periodically in the form of additional tokens of the staked asset. The reward rate can vary depending on the specific asset and network.

4. **Flexibility**: Binance Staking offers various staking options, including fixed-term and flexible staking. Flexible staking allows users to unstack and access their funds at any time, while fixed-term staking locks up the assets for a specific duration.

5. **Compounding Rewards**: Users can choose to compound their rewards, meaning that the rewards they earn are automatically added to their staked amount. This can lead to accelerated earnings over time.

Binance Savings:

Binance Savings is a feature that allows users to earn interest on their idle cryptocurrencies without the need for active trading or staking. It offers a relatively low-risk way to earn passive income on your holdings. Here's how it works:

1. **Selecting a Savings Product**: Binance regularly offers a variety of savings products, each tied to a specific cryptocurrency. These products typically include flexible and fixed-term savings options, each with its interest rate.

2. **Depositing Funds**: Users can choose a savings product and deposit their cryptocurrency into it. Flexible savings allow users to deposit and withdraw funds at any time, while fixed-term savings lock up the funds for a predetermined period.

3. **Earning Interest:** Once funds are deposited into a savings product, users start earning interest on their holdings. The interest rates vary depending on the product and can change over time.

4. **Automatic Payouts:** Interest is typically calculated daily and paid out periodically. Users can see their earnings in real-time on the Binance platform.

Binance Launchpad and IEOs:

Binance Launchpad is a platform offered by Binance, one of the world's largest cryptocurrency exchanges, designed to facilitate Initial Exchange Offerings (IEOs). An IEO is a fundraising method where cryptocurrency projects and startups raise capital by issuing and selling their tokens directly to investors on a cryptocurrency exchange. Binance Launchpad serves as a launch platform for these IEOs, allowing projects to reach a wide audience of potential investors.

Here's a more detailed explanation of Binance Launchpad and IEOs:

1. Project Selection:

- Binance conducts a rigorous vetting process to select projects that will be featured on the Launchpad. This process includes evaluating the project's team, technology, business model, and compliance with regulatory requirements.

2. Token Sale:

- Once a project is selected, it schedules a token sale event on the Binance Launchpad.

- Investors interested in participating in the IEO need to hold Binance Coin (BNB) in their Binance exchange wallets, as token sales on Binance Launchpad are typically conducted in BNB.

3. Token Allocation:

- During the IEO, the project distributes its tokens to investors who participate by purchasing tokens using BNB.

- The allocation of tokens may vary depending on the project's specific rules and the amount of BNB an investor contributes.

4. Transparency:

- Binance Launchpad aims to provide transparency to investors by disclosing relevant information about the project, including its whitepaper, team, technology, and progress.

5. Security:

- Binance's reputation for security extends to its Launchpad platform. Investors can have confidence that their investments are protected by Binance's security measures.

6. Liquidity and Secondary Market Trading:

- After the IEO concludes, the newly issued tokens are typically listed for trading on the Binance exchange. This provides liquidity for investors who want to buy or sell the tokens on the secondary market.

7. Benefits for Projects:

- For cryptocurrency projects, conducting an IEO on Binance Launchpad offers several advantages, including access to Binance's large user base, marketing support, and the credibility associated with being featured on a reputable exchange.

8. Benefits for Investors:

- Investors in Binance Launchpad IEOs have the opportunity to participate in promising cryptocurrency projects early on, potentially benefiting from price appreciation if the project succeeds.

9. Risks:

- It's important to note that investing in IEOs, like all forms of investing, carries risks. The value of tokens can be highly volatile, and not all projects that conduct IEOs will be successful.

10. Regulatory Considerations:

- Both projects and investors should be aware of the regulatory environment in their respective jurisdictions, as IEOs may have legal implications depending on local regulations.

Binance Coin (BNB) and its utility:

Binance Coin (BNB) is the native cryptocurrency of the Binance exchange, one of the largest and most popular cryptocurrency exchanges in the world. BNB was originally launched as an ERC-20 token on the Ethereum blockchain but later migrated to Binance's blockchain, Binance Chain, as the Binance Coin (BNB).

BNB serves multiple purposes within the Binance ecosystem, and its utility has evolved. Here are some key aspects of Binance Coin's utility:

1. **Trading Fee Discounts**: One of the primary utilities of BNB is to provide users with discounts on trading fees when using BNB to pay transaction fees on the Binance exchange. Users can choose to deduct their trading fees in BNB, which results in a discount. This incentivizes traders to hold and use BNB for their trading activities.

2. **Token Sales on Binance Launchpad:** Binance Launchpad is a platform for hosting initial exchange offerings (IEOs) and token sales. Users can participate in these sales using BNB. Owning BNB allows users to access new and potentially promising cryptocurrency projects early in their development.

3. **Payment for Binance Services**: BNB can be used as payment for various services within the Binance ecosystem, including staking, savings, and even certain merchant payments. Binance has expanded its partnerships and integrations to allow BNB to be used in real-world transactions beyond the exchange.

4. **Cross-Chain Transactions:** Binance Coin also plays a role in facilitating cross-chain transactions between Binance Chain and other blockchains. This allows for interoperability and the movement of assets between different blockchain networks.

5. **DeFi** and **DApps**: Binance Smart Chain (BSC), a blockchain developed by Binance, has gained popularity in the decentralized finance (DeFi) space. BNB can be used on BSC to interact with DeFi protocols and decentralized applications (DApps), similar to how Ethereum's ETH is used on the Ethereum network.

6. **Governance**: BNB holders on the Binance Chain can participate in the governance of the Binance Chain ecosystem. They can vote on proposals and changes to the network, providing a degree of decentralization and community involvement.

7. **NFTs (Non-Fungible Tokens)**: Binance has also entered the NFT space, allowing users to create and trade NFTs using BNB on the Binance NFT marketplace.

8. **Burning Mechanism**: Binance periodically conducts "burns" of BNB tokens, which involves destroying a portion of the circulating supply. This burning process helps reduce the total supply of BNB over time, potentially increasing its scarcity and value.

9

Taxes and Regulations

Tax implications of cryptocurrency trading:

T ax implications of cryptocurrency trading can be complex and vary significantly depending on your jurisdiction and individual circumstances. It's crucial to consult with a tax professional or accountant who is knowledgeable about cryptocurrency taxation in your specific area. However, I can provide you with a general overview of some key tax considerations when it comes to cryptocurrency trading:

1. **Capital Gains Tax**: In many countries, including the United States, the buying and selling of cryptocurrencies are considered taxable events. If you make a profit from trading or selling cryptocurrencies, you may be subject to capital gains tax. The tax rate can differ based on the duration for which you held the asset (short-term or long-term) and your overall income level.

2. **Reporting Requirements:** Cryptocurrency transactions may need to be reported to tax authorities. This can include details of each

trade, including the date, the cryptocurrency involved, the amount, the purchase price, and the selling price. It's essential to keep thorough records of your trades for tax reporting purposes.

3. **FIFO or LIFO Accounting:** Some jurisdictions require you to use specific accounting methods, such as First-In-First-Out (FIFO) or Last-In-First-Out (LIFO), to calculate your gains or losses. FIFO means you sell the oldest cryptocurrencies first, while LIFO means you sell the most recently acquired ones first. Understanding and applying the correct accounting method is crucial.

4. **Taxation of Mining and Staking**: If you mine cryptocurrencies or earn staking rewards, the value of the coins you receive may be subject to income tax. How and when these rewards are taxed can vary by jurisdiction.

5. **Tax Deductions and Losses**: In some cases, you may be able to offset your cryptocurrency trading gains with losses. This can reduce your overall tax liability. However, the rules for deducting losses can be complex and subject to limitations.

6. **Gifts and Donations:** If you give away or donate cryptocurrencies, there may be tax implications. In some cases, you could be liable for gift taxes or be eligible for tax deductions for charitable donations.

7. **Reporting Foreign Accounts**: If you hold cryptocurrencies on foreign exchanges or in foreign wallets, you may need to report these holdings to tax authorities if required by your country's tax laws.

8. **Regulatory Changes:** Cryptocurrency tax regulations can change over time. It's essential to stay informed about updates to tax laws and regulations that may affect your cryptocurrency holdings and trading activities.

9. **Tax Filings**: Ensure that you file accurate tax returns and report cryptocurrency transactions as required by your jurisdiction. Failing to do so can result in penalties and legal consequences.

10. **Consult a Tax Professional**: Due to the complexity of cryptocurrency taxation, it's strongly recommended to consult with a tax professional or accountant who has expertise in cryptocurrency tax matters. They can help you navigate the specific rules and regulations in your area and ensure that you comply with tax laws while optimizing your tax position.

Regulatory considerations:

1. Know Your Customer (KYC) and Anti-Money Laundering (AML) Regulations:

- Many cryptocurrency exchanges, including Binance, are subject to KYC and AML regulations. This means users are required to provide identity verification documents, such as government-issued IDs, to use certain features or make large transactions.

- Understanding the KYC and AML requirements on Binance and other exchanges is essential to avoid potential account freezes or closures due to non-compliance.

2. Tax Regulations:

- Taxation of cryptocurrency gains varies from country to country. It's crucial to understand how your country's tax authority treats cryptocurrencies, including reporting requirements, capital gains tax, and any exemptions for small transactions.

- Failure to report cryptocurrency gains accurately can lead to legal consequences and penalties.

3. Securities Regulations:

- In some jurisdictions, certain cryptocurrencies or initial coin offerings (ICOs) may be considered securities and subject to securities regulations. Trading securities without the necessary licenses and compliance can result in legal issues.

- Keep abreast of developments related to cryptocurrency classifications and regulations in your region.

4. Exchange Regulations:

- Regulations regarding cryptocurrency exchanges also vary by country. Some countries have specific licensing requirements for cryptocurrency exchanges, while others may have no regulations or operate under a "gray area."
    - Ensure the exchange you are using, such as Binance, complies with local regulations and follows security best practices to protect your assets.

5. International Regulations:

- Cryptocurrency regulations are not limited to individual countries. International organizations like the Financial Action Task Force (FATF) have provided guidelines for combating money laundering and terrorist financing involving cryptocurrencies.
    - Cross-border transactions may also trigger additional reporting requirements and regulations.

6. Compliance with Sanctions Lists:

- Some jurisdictions maintain lists of individuals, entities, or countries subject to sanctions. Exchanges like Binance are often required to comply with these sanctions and may restrict trading or transactions involving sanctioned parties.

7. Data Privacy Regulations:

- Regulations like the European Union's General Data Protection Regulation (GDPR) can apply to cryptocurrency exchanges that handle user data. Understanding how your personal information is handled and protected is essential.

8. Consumer Protection Laws:

- Consumer protection laws can come into play if there are issues with an exchange or trading platform. Being aware of your rights and the responsibilities of the exchange in case of disputes is important.

9. Regulatory Changes and Updates:

- Cryptocurrency regulations are evolving, and governments worldwide are continually updating their approaches. Traders should stay informed about regulatory changes that may affect their activities.

Reporting cryptocurrency gains and losses:

Reporting cryptocurrency gains and losses for tax purposes is a crucial aspect of responsible cryptocurrency trading and investment.

Tax regulations regarding cryptocurrencies can vary from country to country, and they can be complex. Below, I'll provide a more detailed explanation of how to report cryptocurrency gains and losses:

1. **Determine Your Tax Status**: The first step in reporting cryptocurrency gains and losses is to determine your tax status. Are you considered a trader, investor, or miner in the eyes of the tax authorities? Different tax rules may apply depending on your status.

2. **Keep Detailed Records**: Keeping accurate and detailed records of all your cryptocurrency transactions is essential. This includes information about each trade or transaction, such as date, time, amount, price at the time of the transaction, fees paid, and the parties involved. It's crucial to maintain these records to calculate your gains or losses accurately.

3. Calculate Capital Gains and Losses:

- **Capital Gains:** Capital gains occur when you sell a cryptocurrency for more than you originally paid for it. To calculate your capital gains, you subtract the cost basis (the purchase price plus any associated fees) from the selling price. If you've held the cryptocurrency for more than a year in many countries, it may be subject to long-term capital gains tax, which is often taxed at a lower rate than short-term gains.

- **Capital Losses:** Capital losses happen when you sell a cryptocurrency for less than its cost basis. These losses can be used to offset capital gains and potentially reduce your overall tax liability.

4. **Account for Crypto-to-Crypto Trades:** In many jurisdictions, trades between different cryptocurrencies are also considered taxable events. You need to calculate the fair market value of both the cryptocurrency sold and the one received at the time of the trade to determine the gain or loss.

5. **Reporting to Tax Authorities**: Depending on your jurisdiction's rules, you may need to report your cryptocurrency gains and losses on your annual tax return. This often includes a specific section or form for reporting capital gains from investments.

6. **Keep Updated on Tax Laws**: Cryptocurrency tax regulations are evolving, and new laws may be enacted. Stay informed about any changes in tax laws related to cryptocurrencies in your jurisdiction to ensure compliance.

7. **Seek Professional Advice:** Due to the complexity of cryptocurrency taxation, it's advisable to consult with a tax professional or accountant who specializes in cryptocurrency taxes. They can help you navigate the tax code and ensure you're reporting your gains and losses accurately.

8. **Use Cryptocurrency Tax Software**: There are also cryptocurrency tax software tools available that can help you automate the process of calculating and reporting your gains and losses. These tools can import transaction data from exchanges and wallets, making the process more manageable.

10

Security and Risk Management

Securing your Binance account:

Securing your Binance account is of paramount importance in the world of cryptocurrency trading, as it helps protect your funds from unauthorized access, theft, and other security threats. Here are some key steps and practices to secure your Binance account:

1. **Enable Two-Factor Authentication (2FA):** This is perhaps the most crucial step in securing your Binance account. 2FA adds an extra layer of security by requiring you to provide a one-time code generated by a mobile app (such as Google Authenticator or Authy) in addition to your password when logging in. To enable 2FA on Binance, go to your account settings and follow the instructions to set it up.

2. **Use a Strong, Unique Password**: Ensure that your Binance password is long, complex, and unique to your Binance account. Avoid using easily guessable information like birthdays or common

phrases. Consider using a reputable password manager to generate and store complex passwords securely.

3. **Beware of Phishing Scams**: Be cautious of phishing attempts where malicious actors impersonate Binance or other trusted entities to trick you into revealing your login credentials. Always verify the URL in your web browser and never click on suspicious links in emails or messages. Use bookmarks or type the official Binance website URL directly into your browser.

4. **Email Security:** The email address associated with your Binance account is a critical point of vulnerability. Ensure that your email account is well-protected with a strong, unique password and 2FA. This is because a hacker gaining access to your email can potentially reset your Binance password.

5. **Withdrawal Whitelists:** Binance allows you to set up withdrawal whitelist addresses. This feature restricts withdrawals to specific addresses you have previously approved. Enabling this can add an extra layer of security by preventing unauthorized withdrawals.

6. **Regularly Monitor Your Account**: Periodically check your Binance account for any unauthorized activity. Binance provides account activity logs that you can review. If you notice any suspicious activity, change your password immediately and contact Binance support.

7. **Secure Your Devices**: Ensure that the devices you use to access your Binance account, such as your computer and mobile phone, are secure. Use up-to-date antivirus and anti-malware software, and keep your operating systems and applications patched with the latest security updates.

8. **Binance API Security**: If you use Binance APIs for trading or other purposes, make sure to secure your API keys. Only provide API keys to trusted applications and services, and regularly review and revoke any unnecessary keys.

9. **Personal Information Security:** Avoid sharing personal information on social media or other public platforms that could be used to target you in phishing attempts or identity theft.

10. **Backup and Recovery**: Consider setting up account recovery options in case you ever lose access to your account. This might include using trusted friends' contact information or other verification methods offered by Binance.

11. **Educate Yourself**: Stay informed about the latest security threats and best practices in the cryptocurrency space. Binance often provides security tips and updates on its official website and social media channels.

Recognizing common scams and frauds:

Recognizing common scams and frauds is a critical skill for anyone involved in cryptocurrency trading or investment. The cryptocurrency space has attracted various malicious actors seeking to exploit unsuspecting individuals. Here are some common scams and frauds to be aware of and how to recognize them:

1. Phishing Scams:

- **What it is:** Phishing involves fraudulent attempts to obtain sensitive information, such as usernames, passwords, and private keys, by posing as a trustworthy entity.

- **How to recognize it:** Be cautious of unsolicited emails, messages, or websites that ask you to provide personal or financial information. Check the website's URL carefully for typos or variations from the legitimate site's address.

2. Ponzi and Pyramid Schemes:

- **What it is:** These fraudulent investment schemes promise high returns to early investors by using funds from later investors. They often collapse when there are not enough new investors to pay returns.

- **How to recognize it**: Be sceptical of investment opportunities that guarantee high returns with little or no risk. Research the company and its business model. Legitimate investments come with risks, and returns are not guaranteed.

3. Fake ICOs (Initial Coin Offerings) and Token Sales:

- **What it is:** Scammers create fake ICOs or token sales, often with enticing promises, to raise funds and disappear with investors' money.

- **How to recognize it**: Verify the legitimacy of the project by checking for a credible whitepaper, team members, and community support. Avoid investing in projects that lack transparency or have suspicious information.

4. Impersonation and Fake Social Media Accounts:

- **What it is:** Scammers impersonate well-known figures or crypto influencers on social media platforms to promote fraudulent giveaways or investment opportunities.

- **How to recognize it**: Always double-check the authenticity of social media accounts. Official accounts are usually verified with a blue checkmark. Be sceptical of messages or posts that ask you to send cryptocurrency in exchange for more significant returns.

5. Fake Wallets and Exchanges:

- **What it is:** Malicious actors create fake cryptocurrency wallets or exchanges to steal users' funds.

- **How to recognize it**: Only use well-known, reputable wallet and exchange services. Verify the authenticity of the website's URL and ensure it uses HTTPS encryption. Research user reviews and feedback before using a new service.

6. Pump and Dump Schemes:

- **What it is:** Scammers artificially inflate the price of a low-cap cryptocurrency (pump) to attract unsuspecting investors and then sell off their holdings (dump), causing the price to crash.

- **How to recognize it:** Be cautious of sudden price spikes in low-volume cryptocurrencies. Do thorough research before investing in any asset, and don't follow blindly when someone promotes a specific coin.

7. Malware and Phishing Wallets:

- **What it is:** Malicious software or fake wallet apps are designed to steal your cryptocurrency private keys or funds.

- **How to recognize it**: Only download wallet apps from official sources (e.g., app stores) and be cautious of suspicious links or downloads. Use strong, unique passwords and enable two-factor authentication wherever possible.

To protect yourself from these scams and frauds, it's crucial to stay informed about current threats and exercise caution in all your cryptocurrency-related activities.

Dealing with security breaches:

1. Immediate Action:

- If you suspect or confirm that your Binance account has been compromised, the first step is to act swiftly.

    - Log out of all active sessions on your Binance account from the account settings.

2. Contact Binance Support:

- Notify Binance's customer support immediately about the breach. You can typically do this through their official website or support channels.

    - Provide them with all the relevant information about the breach, such as when you noticed it and any unusual account activity.

3. Change Passwords:

- Change the password for your Binance account immediately, and make sure it's a strong and unique one.

   - Consider changing passwords for associated email accounts and other linked services to prevent further unauthorized access.

4. Enable Two-Factor Authentication (2FA):

- If you weren't using 2FA before, enable it immediately after changing your password. This adds an extra layer of security to your account.

   - Binance offers several 2FA options, including SMS authentication, Google Authenticator, and hardware security keys.

5. Review Account Activity:

- Carefully review your account activity and transaction history to identify any unauthorized or suspicious transactions.

   - If you spot any, report them to Binance and follow their instructions for disputing or resolving unauthorized transactions.

6. Secure Your Devices:

- Ensure that the devices you use for accessing your Binance account are secure. Update your operating systems, install security software, and run malware scans.

- Be cautious of phishing attempts and suspicious emails, and avoid clicking on links or downloading attachments from unverified sources.

7. Monitor Your Financial Accounts:

- If you use the same email and password combination for other financial accounts, change those passwords as well to prevent further breaches.

- Keep a close eye on your bank accounts and credit cards for any unauthorized transactions related to the breach.

8. Report to Authorities:

- In some cases, particularly if the breach involves significant financial loss or identity theft, you may need to report the incident to your local law enforcement or cybercrime authorities.

9. Educate Yourself:

- Take the breach as an opportunity to educate yourself further about cybersecurity best practices.

 - Learn how to identify phishing attempts, use strong and unique passwords, and stay updated on security threats.

10. Consider Additional Security Measures:

- Depending on the nature of the breach and your security concerns, you might want to consider additional security measures, such as using a hardware wallet for storing your cryptocurrencies or using a dedicated device for crypto-related activities.

11

Advanced Trading Strategies

Margin trading on Binance:

1. What is Margin Trading:

- Margin trading enables traders to borrow additional funds (leverage) to increase the size of their positions in the cryptocurrency markets.

- This allows traders to potentially amplify both their profits and losses.

2. How Margin Trading Works on Binance:

- To start margin trading on Binance, you need to transfer assets (cryptocurrencies or stablecoins) into your margin account.

- You can then use these assets as collateral to borrow additional funds, typically denominated in cryptocurrency or stablecoins.

- Binance offers different margin levels, such as 3x, 5x, 10x, and more, allowing you to multiply your trading position size by the chosen leverage level.

3. Long and Short Positions:

- In margin trading, you can take both long and short positions.

    - Long position: You borrow funds to buy an asset, expecting its price to increase. You profit if the price rises.

    - Short position: You borrow an asset to sell it, expecting its price to decrease. You profit if the price falls.

4. Margin Calls and Liquidation:

- Margin trading involves borrowing funds, which means you must maintain a minimum balance (maintenance margin) to cover potential losses.

    - If your account balance falls below the maintenance margin due to trading losses, you may receive a margin call, requiring you to deposit more funds or close positions.

    - If you fail to meet the margin call, your positions may be liquidated to repay the borrowed funds, potentially resulting in a significant loss.

5. Risk Management:

- Margin trading can be highly profitable, but it's also riskier than spot trading due to the potential for rapid losses.

    - Risk management is crucial. Setting stop-loss orders and taking time to understand the assets you're trading can help mitigate risks.

    - Use leverage cautiously, as higher leverage increases potential gains but also magnifies losses.

6. **Margin Trading Pairs:**

- Binance offers a variety of trading pairs for margin trading, including major cryptocurrencies like Bitcoin (BTC), Ethereum (ETH), and more.

- You can choose from a range of assets to trade on margin, depending on your strategy and preferences.

7. Fees:

- Margin trading on Binance involves interest on borrowed funds and trading fees.

- Interest rates can vary based on market conditions and the asset being traded.

8. Education and Practice:

- Before engaging in margin trading on Binance, it's essential to educate yourself about the risks and strategies involved.

- Binance provides educational materials and demo accounts where you can practice margin trading without risking real funds.

Margin trading can be a powerful tool in the hands of experienced traders, but it's not suitable for beginners or those unfamiliar with the cryptocurrency market's dynamics. Due to the high risk involved, it's crucial to approach margin trading with caution and a well-thought-out strategy.

Derivatives trading and perpetual contracts:

1. Derivatives Trading:

Derivatives are financial instruments that derive their value from an underlying asset's price or performance. In the context of cryptocurrencies, derivatives trading allows traders to speculate on the price movements of cryptocurrencies without actually owning the underlying assets. Here are some key aspects of derivatives trading in the cryptocurrency market:

- **Leverage**: One of the significant advantages of derivatives trading is the ability to use leverage. Leverage allows traders to control a larger position size with a smaller amount of capital. While this can amplify profits, it also increases the risk of significant losses.

- **Hedging:** Derivatives can be used for risk management and hedging purposes. Traders can use derivatives to protect themselves from adverse price movements in the cryptocurrency market.

- **Various Derivative Products**: In addition to perpetual contracts, other common cryptocurrency derivatives include futures contracts, options contracts, and swaps.

2. Perpetual Contracts:

Perpetual contracts, also known as perpetual swaps or perpetual futures, are a specific type of cryptocurrency derivative product. They have gained popularity because they allow for continuous trading without an expiration date. Here are some key characteristics of perpetual contracts:

- **No Expiry Date:** Unlike traditional futures contracts, which have expiration dates, perpetual contracts don't have a set expiry. Traders can hold their positions as long as they want, provided they meet margin requirements.

- **Funding Rates:** Perpetual contracts use a funding mechanism to keep the contract's price in line with the spot market. Traders pay or receive funding based on the contract's premium or discount to the underlying asset's price. This helps prevent large price disparities between the contract and the underlying asset.

- **Leverage**: Perpetual contracts often offer high leverage, which means traders can control large positions with a relatively small amount of capital. However, this also increases the risk of liquidation if the market moves against the trader.

- **Mark Price:** Perpetual contracts typically use a mark price (an average of spot prices from different exchanges) to determine the contract's value and funding rates, rather than relying solely on the last traded price.

- **Liquidation**: Trading perpetual contracts carries the risk of liquidation. If a trader's position moves against them and their margin balance falls below a certain threshold, the exchange may liquidate the position to cover potential losses.

Algorithmic trading and trading bots:

Algorithmic trading, often referred to as algo trading or simply algorithmic trading, is a trading strategy that relies on computer programs and algorithms to execute trades automatically. It involves the use of pre-defined rules and mathematical models to analyze market data, identify trading opportunities, and execute trades at optimal times and prices. Algorithmic trading can be applied to various financial markets, including stocks, bonds, forex, and cryptocurrencies.

Here are some key aspects of algorithmic trading:

1. **Market Analysis**: Algorithmic trading systems analyze large volumes of market data, including price, volume, order book depth, and other relevant information. They use this data to identify patterns, trends, and potential trading opportunities.

2. **Rules-Based Trading**: Algorithms follow specific trading rules and criteria set by traders or developers. These rules can be based on technical indicators (e.g., moving averages, RSI), statistical arbitrage, quantitative models, or other strategies.

3. **Speed and Efficiency:** One of the primary advantages of algorithmic trading is speed. Algorithms can execute trades much faster than human traders, allowing them to take advantage of short-lived market opportunities and respond to market conditions in real time.

4. **Risk Management**: Algorithmic trading systems can include risk management mechanisms to limit losses. These may include stop-loss orders, position-sizing algorithms, and risk-reward parameters.

5. **High-Frequency Trading (HFT)**: High-frequency trading is a subset of algorithmic trading that involves executing a large number

of trades in very short time frames, often measured in milliseconds or microseconds. HFT strategies capitalize on tiny price discrepancies and market inefficiencies.

Trading Bots:

Trading bots, also known as trading robots or automated trading systems, are software applications designed to execute trades on behalf of a trader. These bots can be based on algorithmic strategies or simpler rule-based approaches. Here's more on trading bots:

1. Types of Trading Bots:

- **Market-Making Bots:** These bots place both buy and sell orders around the current market price, aiming to profit from the bid-ask spread.

- **Arbitrage Bots:** Arbitrage bots exploit price differences for the same asset on different exchanges, buying low and selling high to make a profit.

- **Trend-Following Bots**: These bots identify trends in the market and place trades in the direction of the trend.

- **Statistical Arbitrage Bots**: They use statistical models to identify pairs of assets with historically correlated price movements and trade them when deviations occur.

- **Sentiment Analysis Bots**: These bots analyze social media sentiment, news, and other sources to make trading decisions based on market sentiment.

2. Advantages of Trading Bots:

- **Automation:** Bots can trade 24/7 without human intervention, reacting to market movements in real time.

- **Speed**: Bots can execute trades instantly, taking advantage of rapid market changes.

- **Eliminating Emotions**: Bots don't experience fear, greed, or other emotions that can affect human traders' decisions.

- **Backtesting:** Bots can be backtested against historical data to assess their performance.

3. Risks and Challenges:

- **Technical Issues:** Bots can encounter technical glitches, requiring monitoring and maintenance.

- **Overfitting**: Creating overly complex algorithms can lead to overfitting, where the bot performs well in backtesting but poorly in real market conditions.

- **Market Risk**: Markets can be unpredictable, and trading bots are not immune to losses.

- **Regulatory Compliance**: Depending on the jurisdiction, using trading bots may involve regulatory considerations.

12

Future of Cryptocurrency and Binance

Binance's role in the industry:

Binance was one of the largest and most prominent cryptocurrency exchanges globally, playing several critical roles in the cryptocurrency and blockchain industry. It's essential to keep in mind that the cryptocurrency industry is highly dynamic, and Binance's role may have evolved since then. Here are some of the key roles and contributions that Binance had in the industry up to that point:

1. **Cryptocurrency Exchange**: Binance started as a cryptocurrency exchange platform and quickly became one of the most popular exchanges due to its user-friendly interface, a wide range of supported cryptocurrencies, and low trading fees. It provided a platform for users to buy, sell, and trade various digital assets.

2. **Innovation and Expansion:** Binance was known for its commitment to innovation. It regularly introduced new features and services, such as Binance Futures, Binance Launchpad for token

sales, Binance Smart Chain (BSC), and more. These initiatives contributed to the growth and diversification of the cryptocurrency ecosystem.

3. **Global Presence:** Binance expanded its services to users worldwide, offering multiple fiat currency on-ramps and supporting numerous languages. This global presence helped bring cryptocurrencies to a broader audience and increased accessibility for users from different regions.

4. **Binance Coin (BNB):** Binance introduced its native cryptocurrency, Binance Coin (BNB), which initially served as a utility token for discounted trading fees on the platform. However, it evolved into a multi-purpose token, with use cases including participating in token sales on Binance Launchpad, staking on Binance Smart Chain, and more.

5. **Binance Smart Chain (BSC):** Binance launched its blockchain platform called Binance Smart Chain, designed to facilitate decentralized applications (DApps) and smart contracts. BSC aimed to provide a more efficient and low-cost alternative to other blockchain networks like Ethereum, making it attractive for developers and users alike.

6. **Token Listings and Innovation:** Binance was known for its rigorous listing process for new cryptocurrencies, which aimed to ensure the legitimacy and security of assets listed on the platform.

Additionally, Binance frequently supported innovative projects, helping them gain exposure and liquidity.

7. **Education and Research**: Binance invested in educational initiatives and research to promote blockchain and cryptocurrency adoption. This included the publication of research reports, hosting webinars and conferences, and providing educational content for both beginners and advanced users.

8. **Charitable Initiatives**: Binance was involved in various charitable activities and initiatives, including the Binance Charity Foundation, which aimed to use blockchain technology for social good, such as providing transparent and efficient aid distribution.

9. **Regulatory Compliance**: Binance worked to comply with regulatory requirements in various jurisdictions, seeking licenses and partnerships where necessary to operate legally and transparently.

13

Conclusion

In this comprehensive Binance Trading Guide, we've embarked on a journey through the fascinating world of cryptocurrency trading. We've explored the intricacies of Binance, delved into the fundamentals of cryptocurrencies, and dissected various trading strategies. Throughout this journey, we've uncovered not only the potential for financial gains but also the transformative power of blockchain technology and the evolving landscape of finance.

As we conclude our exploration, it's crucial to reflect on the profound implications of what we've learned. The cryptocurrency revolution is not merely about trading for profit; it signifies a paradigm shift in the way we think about money, ownership, and trust. It's a revolution that offers financial inclusivity to the unbanked, challenges traditional financial systems, and promotes decentralized governance.

Binance, as one of the leading cryptocurrency exchanges, has played a pivotal role in this transformation. It has provided a platform for individuals like you to participate in the global digital economy, enabling financial freedom and opportunities for millions worldwide. However, with great power comes great responsibility. As you navigate the crypto landscape, always remember the following key takeaways:

1. **Education is Empowerment**: Cryptocurrency and blockchain technology are complex subjects. Continuously educate yourself and stay updated on the latest trends and developments. Knowledge is your most potent weapon in this space.

2. **Risk Management is Paramount:** The crypto market is known for its volatility. Be cautious and employ risk management strategies to protect your investments. Never invest more than you can afford to lose.

3. **Long-Term Vision**: While day trading can be profitable, consider adopting a long-term perspective. Many of the most successful investors in the crypto space have benefited from holding assets over time.

4. **Security First**: Safeguard your assets with robust security measures. Use hardware wallets, enable two-factor authentication, and be wary of phishing attempts. Your digital assets are your responsibility.

5. **Diversify Your Portfolio:** Don't put all your eggs in one basket. Diversification can help spread risk and increase your chances of success.

6. **Compliance Matters:** Stay informed about tax regulations and legal requirements in your jurisdiction. Compliance ensures that you stay on the right side of the law.

7. **Community and Innovation**: Embrace the vibrant crypto community and contribute to the evolution of this groundbreaking technology. The future of finance is a collective endeavour.

In closing, the world of cryptocurrency and blockchain technology is a dynamic and evolving landscape. It's a space where innovation knows no bounds, and possibilities are limited only by our imagination. As you continue your journey in the crypto universe, remember that you are part of a global movement that is reshaping finance and challenging the status quo.

So, whether you're here for the financial gains, the technological innovation, or the pursuit of a more inclusive financial system, you are a pioneer of the digital age. Embrace this opportunity, stay vigilant, and always strive for a better, more equitable future. The world is changing, and together, we're shaping the future of finance—one blockchain transaction at a time.

Thank you for joining me on this exciting journey. Here's to a prosperous and enlightened future in the world of cryptocurrency and blockchain technology.

Safe trading and happy hodling!

www.ingramcontent.com/pod-product-compliance
Lightning Source LLC
Chambersburg PA
CBHW072216290526
45794CB00004B/1767